To Irene + Tony,
Best wishes,
Chris D.

The Largest Rabbit

Chris Dignam

The Largest Rabbit

First Published May 2014 by

Crafty Dog Books Cymru,

Ti Levran,

59 Capel Road, Clydach,

Swansea, UK. SA6 5PY

www.crafty-dog-cymru.co.uk

First Impression 2014

Second (This) Impression July 2018

ISBN: 978-0-9576932-2-7

Jacket & other illustrations courtesy of Jackie Evans/Jacs Studio

www.jacslittlewelshstudio.co.uk

ACNOWLEDGEMENTS

A special mention has to be made to Sean and Kate Standing who have worked so hard to give so many animals a fabulous home, and then the Mighty Finn, one of their rescues who made so many people's lives brighter by just being Finn.

And to Greyhound Rescue Wales, Galgos del Sol and Donegal Pet Rescue.

DEDICATION

This book is dedicated to all those unsung heroes who have stood on street corners in the pouring rain, howling wind and biting snow to raise money for animal charities.

Especially to Gwyneth and the late Pearl whose contributions were invaluable.

CONTENTS

PROLOGUE

We are not always what we appear to be, and sometimes it takes time for us to become who we want to become. And remember - even the most unlikely of us can become a hero.

This is the story of Rubbish, a rabbit that does not look or act like a rabbit and who becomes the unlikeliest hero of them all!

Chris Dignam, April 2014

1 - DOWN THE RABBIT HOLE

Scutter stopped chewing and raised his head when he heard the car's brakes screeching on the road above. As he looked up from his patch of grass he saw a bundle of brown cloth first fly over his head, and then tumble past him, rolling, rolling, all the way down the bank to the ditch at the bottom. The ball stopped with a thump but the car did not - it continued into the other traffic, horns hooting as it went.

"What's that?" Brownie asked.

Scutter shrugged, "Don't know 'til we go and have a look."

The rabbits turned and shuffled quickly through the shaggy grass and scrubby thistles towards where the flying bundle had landed. It was a rough brown string bag tied with a chunk of equally rough coloured rope.

As they approached the bag it lurched suddenly; the two rabbits leapt backwards in surprise.

"Where am I?" the bag asked in a muffled voice.

Scutter and Brownie looked at each other. "Blimey, a talking bag!" Scutter said to his friend.

"You are on the bank beside the big stream." Brownie spoke slowly, as if he had never spoken to a bag before (which he hadn't) and added, "Welcome to our home."

"I'm hungry…" the Bag said.

Brownie nudged Scutter, "You'd better ask it what Bag's eat."

"Mr Bag," (Scutter assumed from the voice that the Bag was a Mr), "What do Bags eat?"

The Bag moved and sat more upright, the knotted string round its neck looking like a tie. "I'm not a bag."

Brownie shook her head and said to her companion, "He looks like a Bag to me."

The Bag wriggled and the tie around the collar loosened. Seeing the knot coming free, Scutter tugged at it. The Bag shook again and the rope fell off, revealing, as the cloth rolled down, a small head with a small round face and sharp sparkling brown eyes. He was not much smaller than the rabbits, with deep brown fur covered in faint black stripes, a pair of folded ears and a shiny black button nose.

"What are you?" the button-nose wrinkled as he looked at the Rabbits.

"Rabbits of course," Scutter replied. "What are you?"

Button-nose shrugged. "Don't know. I'm just me."

Brownie and Scutter whispered to each other and then Brownie said, "You must be a Rabbit too. You must be from a different warren." (A warren is what rabbits call their home).

Scutter nodded and so did the new Rabbit, joining in.

"So how did you get in the bag?" Brownie asked, kicking at the pile of cloth with her foot. "That's a really clever trick."

"Dunno," the new rabbit answered.

"Where is your home? Are there other rabbits there like you?"

The new rabbit shrugged, "I don't know where I am so I can't say how far I am from home. I live in a shed in a basket." The new rabbit's face brightened, "- perhaps you know it? It's made of wood and smells of…well…rabbits I guess. And it's blue."

Brownie and Scutter frowned and shook their heads, "There's no sheds like that round here. We're on the edge of the small wood." To be fair, they did not really know what a shed was anyway.

"What about the rest of your family?" Scutter enquired.

Again the new rabbit looked a bit awkward. "There's only me. I had brothers and sisters but they've all gone."

Scutter shook his head. He found this difficult

to believe. "What about your mum and dad?"

"I never had a Dad and Mum left us ages ago." As Mr Bag talked he could feel his eyes stinging as tears began to form.

This made Scutter and Brownie feel really uncomfortable, seeing him getting so upset. "Never mind," Scutter said trying to sound bright and buck the little rabbit up a bit, "Come home with us." He put his arm across the new rabbit's shoulder and gave him a hug. Brownie smiled at the sad rabbit too and it made him feel better.

"What's your name; we can't keep calling you Mr Bag as you clearly aren't one," Brownie told him.

"I don't have a name. The people called me lots of things. They said I was rubbish." He paused. "That must be my name."

"Well Rubbish, come home with us and we'll sort out how to get you back to your home."

"Yeah," said Brownie and she too gave Rubbish a hug. "Bluebell will know how to find your home and your family. She knows everything."

Scutter pulled the bag off Rubbish's feet and he stepped out. They hopped together (well, he did not hop like the other rabbits, his was more a sort of walk) down the embankment, along a winding path through the edge of a patch of woodland to the entrance to the warren, a large rabbit hole under an old and spiky hawthorn tree.

"Come on in," Brownie called over her shoulder as she hopped into the tunnel. Rubbish stopped, feeling a bit frightened. "But it's dark…" he said. He shivered a little; Rubbish did not like the dark. He had spent a lot of time on his own in the dark in the shed and it was something he had never got used to. Scutter stood behind him and he gave him a helping shove. Rubbish reluctantly slid and shuffled down the passageway, the other rabbits encouraging him with kind words and gentle pushes. Brownie led the way, Rubbish followed and Scutter trailed behind. He could not help noticing that Rubbish had a short straight tail, nothing like a scut (a rabbit's fluffy tail). He was definitely a different type of rabbit to the rest of them.

Deep down in the burrow (another name the rabbits use for the tunnels they call home) the rest of the rabbits were either dozing or cleaning out their bedding. Rubbish had expected it to be dark under the ground and smell of damp but it was not; it was really quite light and smelled of rabbits; not a dirty smell but more of a welcoming smell of warmth that seemed to wrap itself around you like a comfy blanket. In the centre of the huddle there stood one rabbit much bigger and browner than the others who they all seemed to listen to without any questions. This was Bluebell, the Mother Rabbit who literally ruled this roost. She was calling out orders to everyone as food was brought from distant tunnels and was allocated, fairly, to everyone there.

"And who do we have here?" She turned to face Brownie and Scutter and Rubbish who stood in between them hoping that he would blend into the background.

Rubbish looked down at his feet and just mumbled something. He could feel the eyes of all the rabbits watching him and he could also feel his cheeks get warm as he began to blush under his brown stripes.

"Speak up, I can't hear you." Bluebell prodded.

Scutter answered for him, "His name's Rubbish and we found him dumped by people."

Brownie nodded emphatically, "In a bag, he was tied up in a bag... it was horrible, Mum".

Scutter continued, ignoring Brownie's interruption, "He doesn't know where his warren is. So I said until he can find it he could come here. He has nowhere else to go."

"Oh, has he not?" Bluebell's voice softened. She lifted Rubbish's chin with her paw and looked into his sad brown eyes. "I'll not have any child abandoned whilst I have food and a roof to give them. Welcome to the warren young Rubbish." She ruffled his chin and Rubbish smiled and gratefully answered with a shy, "Thank you very much."

"You can stay here as long as you need to or until we can find your family and get you home. Rubbish…that's a daft name for a Rabbit," said Bluebell shaking her head and tutting, "And you are the strangest looking rabbit I have ever seen." She looked at the skinny little brown and black stripy bunny. His legs looked very long for a rabbit…and then there was that tail…

"Remember that funny fat one we met with droopy ears," one of the other Rabbits said. This rabbit was dark grey, very big and plump and had a deep gruff voice.

"Yes, Dad," said Scutter nodding. "That was Freddy and he said he was a Belgian Lop or something."

"Belgian, huh! He was only from a few fields away, I could tell by the way he talked," replied Bluebell. "Right then everyone, excitement over! Wash your paws and sit to eat," she called out to the warren.

Rubbish washed his paws with a tongue longer and pinker than any of the other rabbits, and then with the rest of the warren sat to eat the food he was so kindly given. It was really nice but not what he was used to - dandelions and carrots and other vegetables. Tasty and crunchy, not like the sloppy boiled up veg he had been given by the people. There the food had been mostly water with a few soft, mushy potatoes and carrots and maybe some green cabbage stalks. The other rabbits all ate away though Rubbish could feel each of them in turn looking at him and he could hear the occasional comment about "Big feet," or "Long nose" or even "Big teeth."

2 - A HOME AT LAST

Over the weeks and months Rubbish settled in very well. To Rubbish it was so different to the life he had known before. In the shed he had been on his own most of the time, only saw the people once in the morning and then in the evening. They had let him out onto a patch of cement surrounded by high walls where he used to go to the toilet. Then he was put back in the shed. If he was lucky they changed his drinking water, otherwise it had to last a few days. They had fed him in the evening. Nights had been dark and very lonely after his brothers and sisters had left. Here and now, Rubbish was really happy with the other rabbits.

Life in the warren was fairly relaxed. Bluebell was of the opinion that as long as you ate your food, kept your bedding clean and did your share of the chores then life was good and pretty easy. The routine was firstly clean your bedding out, breakfast, then out foraging for food for the warren to share, then back for lunch, do a bit more foraging for food, then back for tea, then a bit of sitting round and talking in the evening before bedtime just as it got dark. Some of the older rabbits went out after dark but the youngsters preferred to come in and get some sleep until the sun came up again – and Rubbish was one of those.

On these evenings Bob or Bluebell or one of the other senior rabbits would tell stories about the history of the family. Some of these stories were of the strange characters they had been related to. Bob used to tell really funny stories about what he had done when he had been a kit (a young rabbit), or of things other members of the family had done. He used to have everyone rolling round in stitches, holding their sides as they ached with laughing so much. Then there were the other stories, the spooky stories that the kits loved to hear, even though they scared them. There were tales of weasels and stoats who raided burrows for food, often taking unsuspecting little bunnies for their supper, of flying owls that spied for little rabbits out on their own at night, watching them from trees with their huge bright eyes. And of the other things that lurked in the depths of the wood, things that he did not dare to name. He would always tell the entranced but terrified little rabbits, "Beware of the things that lurk in the deep dark wood. There are things with teeth and claws that are just waiting for a lost and lonely rabbit. Whatever you do, stay close and make sure you are home well before dark." He would look around at the young rabbits sitting around him, their eyes wide with awe and fear. Some of the older rabbits did not believe this was true, or only in part. Sometimes Bob would beckon them to come closer, and as they leaned in, he would look from side to side, lean closer to them and then go, "BOOO!" The little rabbits would leap out of their skins and laugh as well as shake a bit too!

Rubbish discovered that there were fifteen or sixteen of them living in the warren, mostly Bluebell's children but with a few Uncles and Aunties and cousins. They were mainly youngsters, brown and white but a few with grey fur coats. Despite all the variety in colour and size, none of them looked anything like Rubbish. But, everyone was very friendly and took to him so well; maybe in large part because of his terrible background and the way he had found himself here.

Bluebell became especially fond of Rubbish and took particular care of him – she felt that of all her children, Rubbish was the one who needed mothering most. One day he had told her about his brothers and sisters back in the shed - there had been five others, he could remember them, but one of them had been very weak and one morning when they woke he was not there. The others had one by one been picked up by other people until he was the only one left in the shed. He had not liked it on his own, sitting in the cold dark shed on his tiny scrap of blanket, waiting for the door to open. He used to wish to himself that maybe someone would come and collect him too and take him to a home. Rubbish had been so excited when they had come for him, picked him up and took him outside into the big shed with wheels on that rumbled and roared as they went down the street. He remembered looking from the person's lap at other wheelysheds flying past, some in the same direction, some the other way. The people were very noisy and harsh and did not speak very nicely to him, not like Bluebell and the rabbits now did. He told Bluebell how one of them had pulled a cloth from behind their seat and put it over Rubbish and tied him up – that had been the dirty sack they had found him in. After that he remembered being even more frightened and he had shivered with fear as they rumbled on, then he heard a door open and felt himself being lifted up, then flying and tumbling down, down until he had come to a halt and heard Scutter and Brownie.

Rubbish had cried the first time he told Bluebell about this; he could remember and feel how miserable, lonely and scared he had been and Bluebell had comforted him. "Hush, little bunny, you are safe now, and we all love you." Rubbish had never heard that word before – he had never known what it was to be cared for, and had never felt loved. This was the best feeling in all the world. After the horrible things that had happened to him, Rubbish at last felt that this was the place he really belonged.

Bluebell had sat with Bob that evening and they had talked about this strange little rabbit and where he had come from. They had heard stories about the people keeping rabbits in little sheds and occasionally one escaped. They knew of a few of these escapees. Some were brown, like them, and some white or black and white. Some had had long floppy ears but they did not have Rubbish's stripes or his funny tail. Bob had suggested that his legs were more like a hare and maybe that's what he was? Bluebell was unsure. The one thing she was certain of was that Rubbish was definitely one of the family.

Every evening just before bedtime, they had roll-call outside the warren. All the kits would line up and

Bluebell would call their names. It was a fairly orderly line of rabbits but as you looked along the row there was one rabbit that stuck out more and more from the rest; as the weeks went by, Rubbish was getting to look less and less like the others.

It was true. Rubbish's legs were getting longer as was his tail and his nose - he was getting pointier at both ends! Out playing one day he had been so happy that his tail wagged and knocked Benjy (one of Scutter and Brownie's brothers) off his feet!

They joked about his being so gangly; as his legs grew Rubbish would trot down the corridor and trip some of the others up or fall over his feet himself. Three legs would go one way and one leg would go the other (it did not matter which leg and it seemed each one tried it at different times). When it was time for tea the other rabbits would all bounce into the chamber and Rubbish would invariably come rolling in, head over heels, apologising as he came, scattering rabbits as he bowled past. He was getting tall and lanky and very clumsy.

Over the months his nose grew even quicker than his legs and he would inevitably get it stuck in places it should not necessarily have been. It did not help that his nose often arrived a few seconds before the rest of him. One afternoon they had all been playing in the woods and Scutter and Scamp had found a tree with a hole in the bark. They had looked through the hole from both sides as part of a game but when Rubbish had tried to look he had managed to get his nose stuck. It took Scamp pushing and Scutter pulling to get Rubbish's black button nose free (all the while he was telling them to be careful as his nose was very delicate but they took no notice, just pushed and shoved)! But no matter how much he grew and changed, they all still accepted that though Rubbish was an odd rabbit, he was one, and one of the family.

.

3 - RUN RABBIT RUN

It was great to have friends, especially to play with. All the rabbits loved to go out onto the short grass of the meadow (it had recently been mown for hay) and there they liked to have races. Brownie was one of the fastest of the rabbits, despite her being quite small. Rubbish would sit and watch the other rabbits running the length of the meadow but he never really felt inclined to join in....until that is, the day that it just clicked. He was lying on his belly with his chin on his front feet and watching them scamper about when two of the rabbits ran across in front of him as he dosed off. Suddenly Rubbish's ears stuck up, his body pulled him bolt upright and before he knew what he was doing he was off! He ran across the meadow, gently at first and then opening up and stretching his body to its full length as he ran. He flew past the other rabbits and just continued around the whole of the meadow like a flying brown stripy rocket. Many of the rabbits just stopped where they were and stared, some open-mouthed, as Rubbish flew past. They had never seen a rabbit run like this and never quite as fast. It was amazing. Rubbish drew to a halt, puffing and panting, but it had felt so good to run like that. His heart was pounding; he was so happy and so alive.

"Well, well, Rubbish – that was really fast," Scutter said trotting up to him. "We never thought you had it in you."

Rubbish stared down his long legs to his feet at the farthest end, "To be honest, neither did I!"

"You are almost as fast as Brownie," another rabbit said.

Scutter shook his head. "I think he's faster."

Brownie had skipped over and was looking at Rubbish in awe.

"OK," she said to Rubbish. "Try and pass me!" With that she sped off across the grass.

Rubbish took a deep breath and launched himself after the little rabbit who was a tiny blur disappearing across the field. Within thirty long, ground-clutching strides Rubbish had caught up and they ran alongside each other. Rubbish was laughing as was Brownie, slightly breathlessly. They could hear the others cheering in the distance as Brownie took a deep breath and speeded off again. Rubbish grinned and just increased the length of his stride too. He caught up and then passed Brownie and whizzed on around the edge of the field and back to where the group of rabbits were gathered. Others had come now and they were all cheering the two of them as first Rubbish skidded and Brownie bounded to a halt.

There was a lot of chattering between the rabbits. You could hear them saying, "Amazing" or "Outstanding" or "He can fly!" Rubbish had a good shake and turned to give Brownie a kiss. "That was really fun," he told her. "I've never run like that before."

Brownie was smiling too, "I never thought anyone would ever catch me, let alone overtake me and shoot off into the dust! You can run really fast, can't you!"

Rubbish shook his head, "I just don't know where it came from. All of a sudden my legs just took off and my body, well, just followed."

"Very quickly!" added Brownie.

Scutter laughed so much he fell over. "Rubbish, you are the most surprising rabbit I've ever seen!"

As the weeks went by, Rubbish began to notice that he was having problems getting in and out of the entrance of the burrow. He even told Scutter that he thought the doorways were getting smaller. Scutter shook his head, "Don't be silly Rubbish – it's you! You are growing so much."

Bob the big rabbit, Scutter's dad and Bluebells husband, called a meeting one day of all the rabbits. "Family, we are having a slight problem. Our little Rubbish is not as little as he once was," he looked up at Rubbish who had to bend and squash himself to fit at the end of the main hall in the warren, "and so we will have to do some building work. I have been thinking and decided we should widen some of the main tunnels, the big sleeping chamber and the Hall, here." Many of the rabbits commented, "Yes" or "True" or "Good idea". "And as young Rubbish appears to be growing even more, we should consider building him a door of his own, under the bracken at the end of the hill, so he can come in and out easier."

There was a sea of nodding heads and a chorus of, "Bravo!" or "Great!" or even "Wish I'd thought of that!" Over the next three weeks the rabbits worked at widening and building. Bob had a large nut shell which he had fashioned into a helmet which he called his "Building Hat" and this is what he wore when he was directing the work. He clearly enjoyed this part of his responsibility; warren leader and chief builder! As the weeks went by the main hall became far more spacious and the work then began on Rubbish's own entrance. There was a thick clump of bracken at the end of the bank and this was where Bob had identified the perfect spot to build Rubbish's doorway. It was tall and wide enough for Rubbish to be able to wriggle in without any problems (or getting wedged as he had recently done) and the bracken hid it from view. Rubbish's own secret doorway. As Bob cut the rope made of grass to declare the entrance "Open" he ushered the rabbits and Rubbish down the new corridor and at the end, just next to the Main Hall there was now a large curtain. Bob and Bluebell together gripped the bottom corner and pulled it back. Inside was a large room with a thick layer of straw bedding and a white towelling sheet. Bluebell was beaming, "This is your very own room and your own bed! No more lying with the others and your feet sticking out of the bottom of the blankets!"

Rubbish was so pleased he could not find any words; he just kept saying, "Wow...is this mine? Wow!"

All the other rabbits came in to see the huge cavern that was Rubbish's room. Brownie nudged him, "We found the blanket up in the meadow beyond the woods. It took four of us ages to drag it back."

"Cor, thanks Brownie," Rubbish smiled, "My own bed. Wow!".

4 - RUBBISH TO THE RESCUE

The summer seemed to be really magical; lovely long sunny days, sitting out in the warm sun, chewing grass, watching the birds hopping from tree to tree. Yes, Rubbish was convinced this was the best life anyone could ever have. Not a worry in the world. Sometimes (in spite of Bob's warning tales) the young rabbits would wander a bit further from the warren into the wood where there were patches of especially nice grass, or nice mushrooms or tasty tree bark. Once they had come across a young deer who had stopped for a chat. She had been very nice, a bit shy but friendly and very curious about this big rabbit. Rubbish had wondered if they had been related because her legs were long and spindly like his but her tail was not as long.

Sometimes they played hide and seek. Rubbish loved this game but it was not really a challenge as no matter how hard the rabbits hid themselves he could smell them a mile off and could even tell who it was, as to him they all smelled different. If he was hiding, the others could never find him as they reckoned they could not smell him unless he was upwind and the breeze was blowing straight from him to their noses! It was on one of these hide and seek sessions that Rubbish discovered that not everyone in the woods was nice and friendly.

Scamp was one of the biggest of the other rabbits and he was a bit of a bruiser; he loved the rough and tumble and would thump you on the back when saying "Hello there!" knocking your breath out, and he loved shaking you powerfully by the paw. It was his turn to "Seek" so Rubbish, Scutter, Brownie and three other rabbits scampered into the bushes/behind logs/under the bracken as Scamp counted up to fifty. This could take a bit of a while as he was not the best at counting.

Rubbish found a spot in a clump of wet bracken that hid his scent just in case Scamp decided that day that he could pick up his smell. He squatted in the short grass and leaves and waited to be found. As he lay there he heard voices he had not heard before. There were two voices; rather high pitched, sharp and mean sounding, Rubbish thought. They were talking about the other rabbits and not in a nice way. Rubbish strained his ears to hear what they were saying.

"Yeah, there's about five of 'em," said Voice One.

"From that burrow in the meadow. Big ones and small ones," said Voice Two (this voice sounded even meaner that the other one).

"We could grab one or two and take them back," said Voice One.

"Yeah, could do. Something nice and tender and tasty to eat," said Voice Two. "Is there anyone round to see us?"

"Nah, just a bunch of little bunnies," Voice One sniggered, "No match for us."

Rubbish's ears pricked up. He could smell them quite strongly now, musky and thick smelling, like old leaves and muddy feet. He tried to look through the gap in the bracken but was worried he might make the branches move and warn them. He could feel the hackles, the hair along the back of his neck, rise and his front lip began to curl.

He listened as the two voices spoke about

waiting and then taking the two little fat rabbits that were hiding behind the log away to their left. Rubbish knew that was Brownie and her younger sister Jess. He heard the two voices go quieter and then move away, the grass rustling as they made their way into the undergrowth.

Rubbish was angry. Right then! No-one was going to hurt his family like they had hurt him, that was for sure. He lifted himself off his haunches but still keeping a low profile he slinked though the bracken, keeping the nasty voices between him and the log where the rabbits lay, unaware of the danger. As Rubbish came round he could see through a gap in the scrub. Ahead of him was the log, and the two girls sat with their backs to him, for they were watching Scamp as he counted past 40 up towards his total. Between the rabbits and Rubbish were two very large weasels, evidently the owners of the nasty voices. They slithered closer to the rabbits, as Scamp could be heard counting (slowly) closer to 50.

As Scamp hit fifty, the girls giggled to each other, he shouted, "Coming ready or not!" and it all went off like an explosion. The Weasels sped forward towards the rabbits and made to grab them, the rabbits screamed and jumped into the air but before the weasels reached them Rubbish leapt! He flew at the Weasels, a brown blur, barking loudly as he came. The rabbits had turned and were facing the weasels, their backs pressed into the log, holding hands in terror. The weasels halted and turned around to see what the commotion was behind them; their jaws dropped and their eyes practically popped out with fear and surprise. All they could see was a huge leggy shape, all tongue, claws and big teeth.

"Oops," said Voice One as Rubbish grabbed him in his jaws, shook him and threw him into the air. Number Two watched as his colleague spun up into the tree above. Number Two swallowed and closed his eyes as he too was lifted bodily off the floor, shaken and thrown the other way deep into the bracken.

"And let that be a lesson to you," shouted Brownie.

"Yeah," called Jess. "Don't mess with us or our big brother will duff you up!"

Rubbish stood with his back to the Rabbits

staring out at where the Weasels landed, growling.

"Blimey, what was that," Weasel One called from the tree as he dropped to earth. Weasel Two dragged himself out of the bracken and they helped hold each other up, battered and bruised though they were. "So sorry, sir," Number Two said, in an apologetic (though slimy) voice.

"Bit of a misunderstanding," Weasel One said, tipping his imaginary hat, "We meant no harm."

"Yeah, just playing," said Weasel Two.

They quickly made their exit, backing away, still facing Rubbish and the Rabbits all the while as they slipped back into the undergrowth until they were gone.

Just then Scamp's head appeared over the log, "Found you! You're 'It' !"

Brownie, Jess and Rubbish looked at each other. And laughed!

As they all walked back to the warren they chatted, giggled and told stories about what had happened and how Rubbish had jumped out and saved them. At the edge of the burrow Rubbish stopped and the others continued. He suddenly realised something;

when he had run at the weasels he had made a strange sound without thinking. He had barked. Rubbish had never made that sound before. What a strange Rabbit he must be. Rubbish shook his head...then went in to lunch.

Across the woods two very battered and bruised weasel brothers limped home, wincing and groaning as they went.

Vic (Number One) was using a small branch as a crutch to help him walk. Nev (Number Two) had some moss bandage wrapped round his head. They had walked in silence most of the way back to their den, all the while wondering how they were going to tell their Boss they had been attacked by rabbits.

Just like Rubbish, Nev also had that sudden realisation.

"Oi, Vic," he nudged his brother.

"Ow, it hurts!" Vic answered. "What?"

"That Rabbit, the big one with the teeth," said Nev. "Did you notice anything?"

Vic scowled painfully, "I couldn't see much as I was flying up into a tree!"

"He barked."

Vic shrugged, "So what?"

Nev stopped and looked into his brother's face. "Rabbits don't bark."

Vic thought a while. "Good point. They don't normally attack helpless businessmen like us either. But he bloomin' well did."

"True," Nev replied. He dismissed all thoughts and into the earth they went. "Boss?" he called out. "We're back, but you're not gonna like it."

5 - THE MIGHTY FINN

Rubbish was the hero of the warren for weeks after that. If they had loved him before, they now loved him ten times more, it that was at all possible. He had extra helpings of dandelion soup, wild parsnips and mushrooms and even wild cherries and some apples. However, it was no use. No matter how much dandelion soup, carrot pie and blackberry ice cream he ate, Rubbish still had a craving for something different.

One afternoon, tummy rumbling a bit, he found himself on his own wandering into the woods for a rummage and he came upon an overgrown path he had never noticed before. It led away from the warren, deeper into the woods. There were more brambles here, though they seem to have been pushed aside by something quite big. Here and there were tufts of grey hair caught in the thorns or sharp branches. Rubbish sniffed at it; it didn't smell like rabbit, or weasel for that matter. He walked onwards, a bit more reluctantly in case he ran into the animal that had left this trail. The path continued through the wood until the trees grew fewer and he came to the edge of the trees where he stopped. Ahead of him there spread out a wide stretch of rough grass and beyond it was a red-brick wall, five or six times Rubbish's height (at least, that's how it looked to him). In the middle of the wall was a wooden gate, very tall and narrow, but with a convenient hole at the bottom. Rubbish stepped out of the wood, sniffed the air, and then trotted across towards the gate. The funny smell he had noticed in the wood was a bit stronger now, but by this stage Rubbish was feeling very brave. He stuck his head through the hole at the foot of the gate.

Inside was a garden. A path led straight ahead towards a house which looked similar to the one that he had lived in – well, the one he had lived behind in a shed. There were a couple of sheds here too, including one made of glass. Apart from the heavy smell of animal there was something else he could pick up on the air which smelt really attractive. Rubbish sniffed and snuffled in a deep breath. It was food but it did not smell of vegetables. It was soooo tempting. He could see a bowl just up near the house and it was from this that the lovely tasty smell was coming, he was sure of it. Rubbish plucked up some extra courage and decided that he must give it a closer look.

The hole in the gate was just wide enough to squeeze through and high enough to get under so, breathing in, he pushed and wriggled himself through the gap. There was almost a popping sound as Rubbish sprung out of the gap the other side into the garden. He looked around. It was surrounded by a high wall, again of red brick which had moss and grass growing all over and through it. The path was of hard stone with gaps where clumps of weeds had shoved their way through and were muscling their way along the cracks looking as if they were marching up towards the house, beckoning for Rubbish to follow them.

Rubbish crept up the path, keeping low and doing his very best not to make a sound. When his feet made the occasional crunch, he froze, waited, and then continued. At one point the wind blew and rattled some clothes on a long string that stretched over Rubbish's head. He closed his eyes and waited for something to happen…..but nothing did. As he crept towards the bowl he could see an old rug on the lawn across from the food bowl. Again, he stopped and sniffed – ok, it was just a rug. He heaved a sigh of relief, and relaxed. He was nearly at the bowl now. What was in the bowl was dark, and smelled very rich, and there was juice….

Rubbish leaned forward and pushed his nose into the bowl and wrapped his tongue and his mouth around the lovely chewy lumps. It was absolutely fabulous…he had never tasted anything like this before; it was much nicer even than anything he had eaten in the burrow. He swallowed hungrily; he had not realised how much the rabbit food had been missing this certain something that was certainly not a vegetable.

As he filled his mouth for the third time Rubbish had that strange feeling that someone was watching him. A sound made him stop in mid chew.

"Are you enjoying my dinner, youngster," a voice asked. It was a deep voice, with a soft accent, not unfriendly but with a definite tone of authority.

Rubbish stopped chewing, opened his mouth and let the food fall back into the bowl. He looked round sheepishly and saw the owner of the voice as well as of the bowl of food. It was the rug talking.

The rug was in fact a very hairy animal, like a rabbit but much, much bigger, with four long legs like a deer but covered in thick grey scraggy hair.

"I'm very sorry, sir" Rubbish apologised. He lowered his head and dropped his shoulders in his best "I'm sorry" manner. "But it smells so nice….I've never eaten this before….I never knew it was anyone's...Honest…if I knew it was yours, sir…."

The rug stood up and shook noisily. He was easily four times as tall as Rubbish and gazed down at him through a pair of sparkly and kindly deep brown eyes. "Oh, that's ok, young pup. Fill your belly." The rug chuckled, "Looks like you need it more than I do. Go on – there's plenty more where that came from!"

Rubbish did not need to be told twice. He cleared the bowl within a minute. Behind him he could hear the rug laughing. After licking the metal bowl clean Rubbish looked up into the smiling face…and burped. "Oops, sorry Mr…?"

"I am the Mighty Finn but you can call me Finn" said the rug. "And what is your name, little pup?"

"My name is Rubbish," came the reply.

"That's a funny name for a dog," Finn told him.

Rubbish looked rather puzzled, "What's a dog? I'm a rabbit."

The air in the garden throbbed and shook as Finn laughed a very deep and rumbling laugh that seemed to come from deep within his body and from the drip at the tip of his nose to the fluff at the end of his tail. He shook and shook as he bellowed with mirth.

"My dear young pup, I can assure you that you are not a rabbit but you are in fact a dog, like me," he sat back on his haunches and examined the baffled little Rubbish deeply. "Hmmmm. I think you are also a sighthound like me, but you are not as big and hairy." He mused a while. "I think, my pup, you are a greyhound".

Rubbish was astonished. "What's a greyhound, Mr Finn?" He could not believe his floppy ears. He was not grey and did not feel he was a hound at all.

"Ahum. Let me see...." Finn thought for a while and then announced as if reading from a great book, "A greyhound is a long legged smooth coated dog that can run very fast [Rubbish knew he could outrun the rabbits]. The people," Finn nodded towards the house, "like to race you around a track chasing a metal hare"

At this Rubbish too sat on his haunches copying, without realising, what Finn was doing, he looked at Finn and tilted his head now even more puzzled. "Why?"

"For money," Finn answered.

"Money? What's that?" Rubbish had never heard of money.

Finn explained that money was what people used to get food for his bowl. "I have never seen any actual money, you understand; I leave all that to the

Maid and the Butler. But that doesn't explain about you, young pup. Where have you been, and how did you find yourself here eating my food in my garden on this glorious sunny day?"

"I got to lie down" said Rubbish, feeling rather dizzy as he tried to absorb all this information. He had been suspicious for a while that he was an unusual rabbit but had never thought that he was a dog – after all, Rubbish had never known what a dog was. Ten minutes ago he was happy to be a rabbit but then he had eaten some lovely food and now become a dog, that should be running round chasing a steel rabbit that turned into bowls of food….or something like that. It was a lot for a little bunny or puppy to take in.

He lay down on the grass next to Finn and looking up at him began to tell him his story. He told him about his being in a shed with his family, being parted from his Mum (who he couldn't really remember), the horrible way the people treated them, then the trip in the car, the sack and rolling down the bank to meet Scutter.

Finn sat there and looked amazed at the story

and the adventures so far. He nodded, tutted and laughed in the appropriate places. "Well, well….I must say young Rubbish, that you are the funniest and largest rabbit I have ever seen, and that's the truth!"

"Now I know why I need something apart from rabbit food. I must have to eat dog food as well."

Finn nodded, "It's what you were meant to eat."

Suddenly Rubbish sat up and gasped, "Oh no – Mummy Bluebell will be wondering where I have got to." He ran up the garden, calling back over his shoulder, "Thanks Mr Finn, nice meeting you." He could hear Finn chuckling deeply as he rushed up the grass and pushed his body through the gate but before he ran into the woods he turned and poked his head back through the hole into the garden. "Mr Finn?"

"Yes, young pup," Finn shouted from across the garden.

"Is it ok to come and see you again? For a chat?"

Finn smiled broadly. "Why of course young pup. I can teach you a bit more about being a dog."

6 - THE RABBIT HOUND

Rubbish nodded - then scampered off across the field into the wood and ran as fast as he could down the path towards the warren. He arrived puffing and panting to find an anxious and angry Bluebell waiting at the entrance to the burrow.

"Sorry Mum," he said. "I've been for an adventure."

"Away with you, get in and wash your face and paws."

Pushing into the larger Rubbish sized opening, he said to Bluebell, "And I met a dog".

Bluebell shivered as if a very cold draught had blown past her. "A dog?" She was amazed.

"His name is Mr Finn, and he's really nice." Rubbish made his way into the family chamber.

"Keep away from any dogs young Rubbish, they are dangerous and can eat you up," Bluebell warned him. At the mention of the word "dog" the other rabbits stopped what they were doing and turned towards them.

"Has someone seen a dog?" asked Scutter.

There was a gasp from the rest of the Rabbits.

"I saw one once," shouted Scamp above the noise of all the other rabbits muttering and chattering. "It was as big as a tree and had a mouth full of metal teeth a foot long and its eyes blazed like fire and its tail was as thick as a tree trunk."

There was a chorus of "OOOOhs," and "Awwwwwwws," from the rabbits.

"But Mr Finn was lovely and really kind and he let me eat his food," said Rubbish.

"No good will ever come of dogs," Bob announced.

"People make them chase metal hares round a track," Rubbish told them.

Again there were mutterings and Scutter was nodding, "See, metal teeth and fire to chase metal Hares – I told you!"

That night as Rubbish lay in his bed he had such a mix of ideas and emotions running around in his head. He was taught not to like dogs, but Finn was a dog. If Finn was a dog, he would know if Rubbish was a dog, and so he must be. But if he was a dog, how come he loved the rabbits and this was his home. He did not have metal teeth and he would never chase a metal hare. It was so confusing. He dreamt of giant rabbits breathing fire and with metal teeth and then the rabbit popped open and Rubbish fell out.

After lunch the next day Rubbish quietly wandered off into the woods and made his way back to the door in the wall. He reached the gate and gave a polite cough.

"Come in, young pup," a voice called. "I've been expecting you!" Rubbish popped his head through the gap in the door and there was Finn, lying on a bench under an umbrella at the far end of the lawn. Tail wagging wildly he ran up the garden path towards Finn.

"Hi Mr Finn, how are you doing?"

"Fine my young fellow, how are you?" bellowed Finn. "Come down here and pull up a sofa."

Finn was sitting on a chaise longue (that's what he called it), a sort of long padded table with cushions. Alongside was another one with less padding but also quite comfortable, Rubbish had to admit.

"My Butler and Maid look after me well here," Finn told him. "Would you like a biscuit, young fellow?"

Finn nodded towards a bowl of bone-shaped biscuits in a metal dish that sat on a table between the sofas. "Thank you Mr Finn, I don't mind if I do," Rubbish leaned over, picked up a biscuit and crunched it away.

"Chocolate flavour. I had the Maid buy them specially. It's ok, they're not real chocolate as that can be harmful for dogs. I find them a satisfactory substitute."

"Very nice," Rubbish agreed. "Can I have another please?"

"Help yourself lad, they're there to be eaten. Now tell me what adventures you've had since we last met."

"Not much really but I did have some strange dreams," he told Finn. "The Rabbits tell me dogs are big and vicious and eat rabbits and yet you tell me we are dogs and you are so kind and gentle."

The Deerhound (for that was what Mr Finn said he was) chuckled, "Yes I see you are in rather a dilemma. I am gentle as is most of my breed and I do so dislike raw rabbit. I do my best not to eat bunnies at all though I have been known to chase them a bit but that was in the days before I landed up here. The Butler and Maid ensure I want for nothing so chasing rabbits is no longer required. I do chase the cat from up the way when he climbs into the garden. We both do it for exercise really, you know. He tries to run slowly enough for me to keep up and I do my best not to catch him. We are both getting on a bit, you see. Sometimes we stop for a bowl of milk and a siesta half way through." Finn yawned and crunched another biscuit. "It's all rather civilised here."

"So what should I do?" Rubbish put his head on his paws. He looked deeply worried.

"You have choice and freewill my boy. That means you can decide what you want to do. You can chase rabbits but you choose instead to live with them and protect them." Finn paused to let Rubbish think about this. "After all, there are dogs called sheepdogs that do the same, they protect sheep despite the fact most dogs would love to chase them."

Rubbish looked across at the shaggy grey-haired

old deerhound. He is so wise, he thought to himself. "So I suppose," said Finn, musing some more, "You must be a special type of greyhound – you must be a 'rabbit hound'."

Finn grinned brightly, "Like a sheepdog looks after sheep, a rabbit hound looks after rabbits."

As they sat there the door of the house opened and suddenly there was a person standing there. Rubbish was terrified. His body went stiff with fright.

"Oh, your friend is here," the Lady in the doorway said. "Need any more biscuits, Finn? How about a bowl of milk each?"

Finn winked at Rubbish, "Woof!" he called to the Maid. She went back inside and came out with two bowls of milk. One she placed on the table beside Finn, and the other she placed on the table beside Rubbish. She could see that Rubbish was frightened so she just spoke to him softly, telling him not to be afraid and that no-one would hurt him. She went back indoors.

"Tuck in, young pup," the master told him.

Rubbish needed no more prompting! He remembered this white stuff – milk, she had called it

– from when he had been in the shed but it had never tasted so cold and fresh.

"Mr Finn, this really is a civilised life here. No weasels in your garden."

Finn lifted his head and looked across at Rubbish. "Weasels, you say? I have heard Jeffrey the Cat talking about the weasels. They are always up to no good, young pup. Watch out for them, and also for that Fox."

Rubbish licked milk off his whiskers. "I certainly will Mr Finn. What's a Fox?"

7 - CROSSING A FOX

Far across the forest, under the bramble hedge in the deepest and darkest part, two weasels were being given their orders.

Vic and Nev stood in the earth (this is what a fox calls his home) bowing deeply and promising they would do as they were told and that they would find out what was wanted.

Sitting before them was their boss; a very wise and crafty old fox. His coat was scruffy, like an ill-fitting borrowed old jacket, with some lumps of matted hair and bald patches, the result of encounters with other Foxes. He was always successful in any meetings, though the scar across his brow and the part-closed, blind, white eye suggested otherwise; you should have seen the fox he had argued with! His other eye was clear, sharp and though it sparkled it was very, very cold. His name was Max and he was far older and more cunning than any of the foxes for miles around. With the assistance of the weasels and some others he ran the woodland and countryside around the area as his own business. He ate well, usually when someone had an "accident" and the weasels brought the helpless victim back, usually (bit not always) not alive and kicking. He picked his teeth with a toothpick made from bone (he couldn't remember whose bone it had once been). His attention had been drawn to the rabbit warren some time back. He usually took a couple of old or very young rabbits from the burrows as payment for leaving the rest of their residents alone but this one, this warren, had not delivered for a long time. That's why he had sent "the Boys" around for a visit. Now he was concerned about this "Super Rabbit" that had sent the two weasels packing.

"I am not happy with this turn of events," he had told Vic and Nev. "I am hungry. I will have a couple of young rabbits. Or else", he had looked at the weasels, "I'll eat weasel. It's all the same to me."

He was curious though about this rabbit. It was tall, with big teeth and claws. The weasels were not usually cowardly, but whatever they had seen had scared them almost as much as he did, and the injuries caused had been impressive. Maybe he would pay the warren a visit himself, just to have a look, to see if he could find this rabbit. Max licked his lips. He wondered what Super Rabbit tasted like…..

Max shuffled and clicked his knuckles. "I think I will pay the warren a visit and see this…Super…Rabbit for myself. You two will come with me."

Nev and Vic nodded, "Yes Boss, 'Course Boss" and stepped aside whilst the fox pushed between them and up the passageway out of the earth. They followed closely.

Nev sniggered to Vic. "This should be interesting!"

They came out into a clearing from which a well-worn path led through the woods. The weasels walked beside Max's tail, not daring to push in front of him as they knew their place. They continued in silence, occasionally stopping for Max to listen or nose the air. As they came along a side path Max stopped them and held his claw to his lips to quiet the weasels. They listened, and Max sniffed the breeze. Up ahead someone was coming through the wood on the main path. Max motioned the weasels to lower themselves into the bracken whilst he slinked forward and peered through the shrubbery.

Rubbish had said goodbye to Finn and thanked him for a very pleasant afternoon. After hearing about the metal hare and that he needed to eat some meat, albeit occasionally, Rubbish had been scared that he might sleep-walk in the night and do something awful, like eat Scutter. Finn had found this highly amusing but he had reassured Rubbish that being a rabbit-hound was a good thing, that he was there for a purpose to watch over the warren and that he need not worry about wanting to eat rabbits. The Maid had brought out some dog food for the both of them which Rubbish had enjoyed without being so frightened this time and Mr Finn had come to the garden gate with him to watch him on his way. Rubbish was running all of this through his mind as he trotted through the woods, past the clearing and on towards the warren. He stopped at one point as he thought he could feel someone looking at him but though he looked around carefully he could not see or even smell anyone, so on he went.

8 AN UNFORTUNATE MEETING

Sitting safely back in the undergrowth Max looked at the weasels and smiled a very sharply-toothed smile. "Well, well my boys. It would seem that your Super Rabbit is nothing of the sort. He is just a puppy dog."

"Of course! That's why he barked," Vic pushed Nev, "See, I said that was a funny thing for a rabbit to do."

Nev just rubbed his arm where Vic had nudged him and nodded in agreement. "But what are we gonna do with him? He's fast and got lots of teeth."

Max shook his head, "I too have very sharp teeth, and claws and though not so fast, I am far cleverer than a puppy. Come; let's have a scout round that rabbit burrow." Max ducked back into the bushes and the three villains continued on their way towards the unsuspecting rabbits.

As they crossed through the woods Max could hear the sound of laughing and shouting. He halted the two weasels and beckoned them to follow him on a detour towards these unusual sounds. They headed towards what he knew was a small stream. There, where the stream ran through a very shallow patch, there was a group of squirrels, field mice and a couple of young badgers too. They were splashing in the water and playing very loudly. The Fox and the weasels watched. "What a great opportunity to take a little squirrel for lunch," he whispered to the weasels, "I am feeling a bit peckish". Nev nodded and his brother followed suit. Max looked around the clearing – what would be the best and easiest. There was a high bank at the top of which the fox was lying to watch the antics below; the group of young animals spread out across the level area along the bank of the stream. One of the squirrels was clearly in a world of their own as they were ambling along the riverbank away from the others. Excellent – an easy prey. Max whispered commands to his henchmen who slipped away one left and one right, away from the Fox. Once they were in position, Max moved to the brow of the slope and then stood up. He coughed loudly and dramatically.

The squirrels, mice and badgers stopped their

playing at once and stood, rooted to the spot, looking up at the fox.

"Well, well, well," he called down to the terrified animals. "What do we have here?"

The weasels moved in the background towards the little squirrel standing on their own away from the others.

"My name is Max and I own this forest. You are playing on my land and have not asked for permission."

One of the badgers pushed forward and in his loudest voice (which was not very loud) asked Max, "Mr Fox…is it ok to play here, please?"

Max smiled broadly but his was not the smile of a kindly and happy fox (if such a thing ever existed) but of a ruthless and hungry one. "You may play here, but there will be a price, which I consider quite reasonable."

The animals looked expectantly, wondering what they would have to give the fox to be allowed to keep playing.

The weasels came up behind the lone squirrel and grabbed them, paws over their mouth so they could not cry out, and silently they were gone – along with the squirrel.

Fox was the only one to see this, "Oh, don't worry, I have had all the payment I need just seeing you playing so happily. You may continue."

He stepped back from the edge and disappeared from view. He waited a few minutes until the weasels reappeared with the squirrel who they had gagged so they could not make a sound. From where the three of them gathered around the terrified animal they could hear the young animals beginning to play again.

The three of them were drooling over the squirrel, their saliva dripping on their helpless petrified body. Max was really enjoying this moment.

Across the forest, Rubbish had also heard the animals playing, and he too had turned off the path a bit further ahead of the Fox. As Rubbish headed towards the noise he picked up that strange smell again, and also the smell of those weasels - Rubbish had recognised that scent from their earlier encounter. He could see a scruffy red figure on the bank ahead and had guessed that this was the fox and then he saw the weasels coming back with the gagged squirrel. Rubbish crept forward and moved silently up the path; the fox and the weasels were so intent on the squirrel that they never saw the dog coming closer. As the fox opened his huge, foul mouth to take a bite at the squirrel, Rubbish sprang forward, barking and growling.

The weasels dropped the squirrel as Rubbish got to them, the dog pawing the squirrel away so it rolled backwards to safety. Max, Nev and Vic were so startled that they just stood and watched. Face to face, Rubbish barked as loud as he could and the three of them stepped away from the growling mouth full of doggy teeth….and off the edge of the grass into mid air. Suddenly there was nothing under them.

Shouting and screaming wildly, they rolled down the steep muddy bank towards the stream. The playing animals had heard the noise and scattered to out of the way so the rolling balls of mud that were the fox and his accomplices spun through the mud bath and into the stream with an incredible "splash!" From the edge of the clearing all around came the laughter of all the animals who had seen Max made a fool of. He was furious, but there was nothing he could do as the prey had all scattered, as had the dog and the little squirrel.

Max wiped mud off his coat and face with the help of the weasels and, very wet tail tucked between his legs, he made his way back to his earth. He was furious and absolutely seething with malice. He vowed that he would get his own back on that puppy dog. No-one would make him look like a clown and get away with it.

9 - GOOD DOG OR BAD DOG?

When Rubbish got back to the warren he entered by his private entrance under the bushes. He made his way down the passage and into the main room where the rabbits were gathered and already eating their tea.

"And where have you been, my lad?" asked Bluebell, arms folded and looking particularly stern.

"I've been out," Rubbish answered rather sheepishly. He was going to mention his adventure with the fox and squirrels but just then Bluebell said to him sharply, "You've missed your tea. There's only some dandelion soup and blackberry pie left." Though Bluebell sounded annoyed, this was all just for show as she could never be angry at Rubbish for he was such a sweet boy.

"I've already eaten, thank you very much." Rubbish replied, just as sheepishly.

Bluebell rose on her heels, "Oh? And where would that have been? Was it proper food or have you just been snacking?" Bluebell did not hold with snacking.

Scutter and Scamp stopped chewing and raised their heads to watch what was going on. The less brave rabbits just buried their heads in their bowls and chewed more noisily.

Rubbish smiled. "I've had some grub with Mr Finn."

Bluebell shook her head and pointed her finger, "That dog? What have I warned you about dogs? Rabbits and dogs should never mix."

Rubbish felt a bit ashamed that he had upset Bluebell. He could tell from the chorus of "Dear, dear", "Whatever next" and "Dogs!" from the rest of the family that dogs were not a popular animal around this neighbourhood. This made Rubbish's next sentence even more of an affront to the crowd.

"Mr Finn says that I'm not a rabbit. I'm a dog."

There was an instant silence across the warren, apart from the sound of bowls being dropped, and half chewed carrots falling from mouths.

"What?" Bob asked. "You – not a Rabbit?"

Rubbish shook his head and his ears flapped in a very non-rabbit way.

"A dog?" Scutter repeated.

Rubbish brightened, "But I'm not a bad dog like the others. I'm a good dog – Mr Finn says I'm a rabbit hound"

The rabbits were looking at Rubbish strangely and one or two of the younger kits were beginning to cry. The happy, busy atmosphere seemed to have changed and gone much frostier. The rabbits moved backwards as Bluebell and Bob moved forwards to shield them.

"Rubbish, please will you go to your room. Your father…I mean Bob and I need to speak about something. Go to your room and we will come and see you later." Bluebell was not harsh, but her tone was certainly firm.

"But I just saved some squirrels from the fox," Rubbish added, brightly. The rabbits tutted, and he heard the comments, "Likely story" and "another tale" or "who'd believe him - he's a dog".

Rubbish could not understand what he had done or said that had seemed to upset everyone so much and that they would not listen to him. Feeling hurt he turned and, tucking his long tail between his even longer legs, he made his way into the large chamber with the towelling bed that was his own room. There, he lay down and sighed a very lonely, sad sigh.

All that evening and the next night Max had seethed and boiled when remembering how the puppy had made him look stupid. It was bad enough that Max had been beaten, but in front of all those other animals too. He would be the talk of the forest that night, he was sure. Then the other foxes would find out - it was humiliating. Max did not sleep that night but had paced up and down his earth muttering and cursing to himself. The only thing he could do was to get his revenge on that puppy and win back his reputation for being the evillest and most feared animal in the woods. He needed a way to catch Rubbish by surprise, for that puppy was stronger than he looked and was growing quickly too. The fox decided that he would send the weasels out to have a good look around the warren to see if they could spot any weaknesses. One thing that weasels were good for was creeping about and spying.

That was just what he did the very next morning.

Vic and Nev were to make their way as quietly as they could to the warren and just watch it. When they came back, Max would make a proper decision as to what to do.

Max went with them as far as the wide path. After checking that the coast was clear, he signalled for them to go. Max turned and, whistling silently to himself (for that's how cunning a fox he was that he could whistle a tune and make no sound), returned to his earth to plot some more.

Late in the afternoon the two weasels came back with their report. They had watched the rabbits going in and out the entrance to the burrow most of the morning but they were confused as to how the dog could get in that way because the doorway was so small and narrow. As they were whispering to each other about this, Rubbish had appeared with some of the other rabbits coming back from the wood. They kept their beady, weaselly eyes on him as he had parted from the rabbits and disappeared into the bushes at the other end of the mound.

"That's strange," Vic had commented.

"Yeah," Nev replied. "Where's he gone?"

Vic had slithered over the path and had examined the bushes closely but could see nothing. Suddenly there was a movement and Vic had to freeze as the puppy had popped out of the bush and bounded down the bank. Luckily (for Vic at least) he had not seen the weasel. Vic returned to his brother and they began to follow the puppy. They had stuck with him as close as his own shadow and Rubbish had not suspected they were there; cleverly the weasels had covered themselves with mud and grass which hid their scent so that the unwitting puppy had led them straight back to the secret entrance under the bush. As Rubbish had returned to the mound they watched as he went back into the bushes and pushed them aside to reveal his secret puppy-sized entrance – an entrance, Nev whispered, that would be the perfect size for a fox.

All this was reported to Max, who sat there, smiling broadly and showing off his rows of very sharp (if yellow) teeth. "My boys, I think that we will pay our friends a visit. But not now. We'll go when they least expect it."

The weasels looked puzzled.

"Nice and early tomorrow morning." He smiled again. "I think we'll all have breakfast together."

That had been a strange day for Rubbish. The rabbits had been a bit distant since the revelation that he was not a rabbit but a rabbit hound. Though Scutter, Brownie and Scamp and some of their friends had been fine, some of the uncles and smaller rabbits were not so pleased with Rubbish's doggie announcement. Rubbish had played with the rabbits but somehow his heart was not in it (that was when he had passed the weasels without seeing them and so given away the secret entrance). Rubbish had a terrible night's sleep and was very tired as he sat eating his breakfast the next morning.

Bluebell and Bob and the others were all gathered in the large chamber as they were all given their breakfasts. Rubbish queued with his brothers and sisters and took his bowl of food and sat with Brownie to eat.

Bluebell and Bob were still shocked at what Rubbish had told them and they had been talking about it ever since. As they ate their breakfast Bob had again said, "A dog…why, that's absolutely outrageous. What if he ran amok and ate us all in our beds..."

Bluebell shook her head, "He wouldn't do that. He is just a young rabbit…or puppy."

"No wonder he has such long legs and a funny tail, and big jaws…and huge teeth," Bob was clearly doing a great job of frightening himself.

Bluebell cuffed him around the year, "Pull yourself together, you silly! Rubbish is a good boy, whatever his breeding is. He would not hurt anyone. If this Mr Finn is correct, then he is a rabbit hound and won't hurt us."

Bob was still not happy with this, "How can you take the word of another dog! It's too much of a risk for the rest of us. We can't have a dog living in here amongst us. It's unheard of."

Bluebell reminded him, "Rubbish has had such a horrible life – from the time he was found tied up in that sack he has been nothing but good – he even rescued the children from those horrible weasels – don't forget that!"

In the main chamber the rest of the rabbits were discussing the same thing. Rubbish's friends were of the opinion that he would never eat them, whereas the others kept talking about his huge jaws and teeth, his huge appetite, his being a dog as much as anything else. The littlest kits, the ones that were taught to be frightened of dogs, were just that – terrified.

The subject of the conversations all over the burrow was all the same. Something had to be done about Rubbish. The puppy could hear all this and was feeling even more sad and alone. He put his breakfast bowl down and sighing, crept quietly back to his own room behind his curtain. There he lay curled up in a tight ball wishing he had never mentioned Finn or being a dog.

10 - NEVER CROSS A FOX

Up above on the bank on top of the warren the weasels and Max had been listening to the conversations between Bluebell, Bob and the other rabbits through one of the breathing tunnels that took fresh air into the rabbits' home - but also let sound out. Max was grinning even more than before, and the sight of a grinning fox is not a nice one to behold. For if a fox is grinning, it's because he has something evil on his mind.

"Should we run in and get them now?" Vic whispered, "When they are what you say…preoccupied?"

Max shook his head. "I think this requires a little wait. Let us see what happens."

"Yeah," Nev repeated, "Let's see what happens."

Max told Nev to sneak into the tunnel to take a look round, something that weasels were very good at. He had been made to roll in rabbit poo to hide his scent (Nev had not minded as his cleanliness was not one of his best traits in any case). Once he had a good idea of the layout, he was to come back up to where Max would let his plan unfold.

Nev slid into a side entrance where he could not hear any rabbits - it was fairly overgrown and appeared not to have been used for a few years. He could hear the rabbits talking very loudly, some even arguing, away down the chamber. He continued stealthily as only weasels can. As the sound became louder he slowed, until he came to the end of the tunnel. He realised that what he had come down was one of the ventilation tunnels and this opened up in the roof of the main hall; from where he was he could see down to where all the rabbits, young and old, large and small were feverishly discussing Rubbish. They were so busy talking that they never noticed the weasel looking in and making a mental note of the layout of the room, its ways in and ways out. Nev slithered out backwards, retracing his steps up to the grassy bank above, where the fox and the other weasel waited.

He related the exact look of the room to his brother and his boss, who was clearly deep in thought. When he mentioned the large curtain (which closed off Rubbish's room) the fox laughed in a rather hollow way, as if he knew a joke that he was not quite willing to share at that precise moment. After a few more minutes of thought, Max explained to the weasels exactly how they would tackle the rabbits and the puppy dog.

Rubbish lay in his room feeling very down and more than a little worried. He had loved living with the rabbits and they (so he thought) had loved him. Now that he was not a rabbit any more but a rabbit hound his world had been turned upside down again. He was frightened that he would be put out of the warren; where would he go? What would he do? Rubbish swallowed hard and tried to hold back a tear – he really did not want to leave the rabbits as they were his family, no matter what. They had taken him in, sheltered him and given him protection – after all, that's what a real family was all about.

He could hear talking outside which got a bit louder, then there was shouting. This did not sound good, something was happening. As Rubbish pushed against the curtain to come out of his room it came loose and the next thing he knew there were a load of paws and claws pushing and holding him as the curtain was pulled around him and he found himself being tied up.

As Rubbish had been waiting in his room Nev had carefully blocked the main exit and Vic made his way down the second tunnel. Max had heard about the large entrance made for Rubbish and this is the one he had come down. The rabbits were caught by surprise, Bluebell and Bob in the middle of them. They had all gathered to find out what the mother and father had decided about Rubbish only to find themselves caught in the fox's trap. Leaving Vic to watch over them, Max and Nev had loosened the curtain covering Rubbish's entrance so that as he came through they had bundled him up and with a piece of rope Max always kept round his tail they tied the poor hapless puppy into the sheet of fabric. Once again the poor puppy was wrapped up in a cloth bag. This is what Max had been planning when he had heard Bluebell and Bob talking about how they had found Rubbish and this is the joke that he had thought about and now brought to fruition. The puppy was back in a sack where he belonged!

However, neither the rabbits nor the young dog found it funny.

"So, here we are then." Max eyed the rabbits hungrily.

"Yeah, here we are," repeated Vic.

"Yeah, we are," repeated Nev.

Max flashed them a glare as if to tell them to be quiet. It was dead silent, apart from the occasional sound of one of the kits sobbing, or Rubbish trying to wriggle free.

"Very ironic, I think," the fox sneered. "You were frightened that the dog would hurt you but he was the only one big enough to protect you. Because you would not allow yourselves to trust him, huh, look at him now! He arrived in a sack and in the sack he remains." He nodded towards the struggling bag.

"I'll get you…when I get out of this," the sack wriggled and growled angrily in a muffled way.

"The knot is very tight, dog." Fox spat the word "dog" as if it was something dirty, "You'll not get out of that. Besides, by the time you do we shall have had our fill of rabbit," as Max spoke his mouth watered and saliva dribbled from between his dirty teeth and off his chin. The weasels too could not help but dribble.

Bluebell pushed her way to the front of the rabbits and stood as tall as she could (which was still not very tall). "Leave the children. Eat me first – I am big enough to feed you," she bravely announced.

Max scoffed, "No thank you missus, you are too old and chewy, just like that other one there who is too old and stringy." He pointed to Bob who had stood next to Bluebell to protect the others. "Anyway, I think that as I have you all at my mercy I can take my time and pick and choose who we will eat first. Before this lovely meal I think I will have a nap and a dream of eating rabbit. I'll settle down in that dog's room on his rather comfy looking bed whilst my two colleagues keep you safe and sound. It is very tiring putting a plan like this together and now I can take a rest before my late breakfast or early lunch - I guess you can call it 'brunch'." He glared at the rabbits and they flinched in terror under his steely cold gaze. Satisfied, he reminded the weasels to keep an eye on the rabbits but not to touch them yet. He firmly believed that terrified prey tasted better – the fear helped the meat become more tender and improved the flavour.

However, unknown and unseen, in one of the side tunnels leading down from above a little shape moved; it was Brownie. She had been out for a walk picking flowers so had been late back for breakfast and she had seen the fox and weasels arrive. She crept in as far as she dared to hear what was going on. She was so shocked but she was not sure what to do. Brownie was far too small to do anything on her own; maybe she could try and get to Rubbish – but he was tied tightly up. Where could she get help? Her mind was a blur of ideas which all seemed too stupid to work. Then one of these ideas jumped up from all the others; the other rabbits might not have trusted Rubbish in his choice of friends, but Brownie felt that she could. If they were friends of Rubbish, they were friends of hers. Definitely….or she hoped anyway.

She slipped back up to the surface and then as fast as her rabbit legs could carry her she hopped and ran through the wood. Maybe help would come, from an unusual source but, if Rubbish was right it was the only help they could get.

It seemed to take ages for her to get to where she was going, no matter how fast she ran. She was exhausted when she finally got to the edge of the wood where she could see the red brick wall and the wooden gate. As she approached the gate there was a call from high above her. It was rather a posh but elderly voice and asked, "I say, where are you going to Miss Rabbit? Are you lost?"

Brownie stopped and looked up. Atop the wall sat a plump and balding marmalade cat.

"I am looking for Mr Finn. Does he live here?"

The cat nodded. "What business would you have with the Mighty Finn?" The cat wrinkled his nose and looked down again, "Not lunch are you?"

11 - HERE COMES THE CAVALRY

Brownie looked terrified, "N-no sir," she trembled, "I have come to him for help. A friend of his is in danger."

"Hang on, I'll come down," the cat called. Creaking a bit as he did so, the cat disappeared behind the wall, climbed down and appearing through the hole in the gate, came out (wheezing slightly from the effort) and stood beside the rabbit. He screwed up his eyes so he could see Brownie better. "Awfully sorry, dear, couldn't hear properly from up there. Can't really see much either." The cat grinned a rather gap-toothed but friendly grin, "Old age doesn't come alone, you see?"

Brownie stopped trembling. She could tell that the cat was very ancient, and by the way he moved, was rather arthritic too.

"The name's Jeffrey," he smiled another gummy smile. "How do you do? Come along, little one, I'll take you to meet Finn."

He ushered Brownie through the gap in the

doorway into the wonderful garden that Rubbish had told them about. It looked as amazing as the puppy had described it. Walking up the path Jeffrey the cat called out, "Finn, old chap? Are you able to have a chat with this little rabbit? Says she knows a friend of yours."

Ahead of them there was a shaggy old grey rug, just as Rubbish had described, that suddenly stood up and then shook itself. As Brownie approached, the Great Mr Finn came to meet her and bowed deeply. "Good day, my dear. Now then, don't be afraid. What appears to be the matter?"

Brownie was not afraid of Finn; he spoke in such a calm, deep voice that was magically reassuring. "Mr Finn, sir, I live in the warren with my family. The fox and weasels have come and they are going to eat everyone and they have tied up my brother Rubbish..and ..and.." Brownie looked up at the kindly old deerhound and burst into tears, crying without being able to stop herself.

"There, there, dear child, don't worry. I am sure we can come up with a plan to rescue everyone." From somewhere Finn produced a red spotted handkerchief that he gave to Brownie to wipe her eyes and blow her nose. "Rubbish is in a pickle, eh? See Jeffrey," Finn commented to the cat, "I warned him to watch out for that fox."

"Yes, he's a bit of a cad and a bounder and no mistake." Jeffrey agreed, "Needs to be put back in his place."

"Indeed. We can't have him frightening the rabbits and our little greyhound….I mean, rabbit hound," Finn winked at Jeffrey.

Finn leaned into his bowl and got out a doggie bone biscuit which he crunched loudly.

The cat looked at the deerhound who was deep in thought. "Well, Finn, is it a one biscuit or two biscuit problem?" he asked.

Finn stopped chewing. "Hmm. Definitely a two biscuit problem," he pronounced before helping himself to another biscuit.

The dog stood still as a statue for a few seconds, the gentle morning breeze ruffling his long and shaggy grey coat. Brownie thought as she looked up at him, if ever someone looked like a hero, it was Finn at this moment in the magic garden, sun shining off his coat and reflecting in the sparkles in his deep brown eyes. Jeffrey put his arm across Brownie's shoulders and gave her a hug of reassurance.

"Don't worry, old girl," he told her, "If anyone can rescue them, it's Finn."

"OK – I have an idea!" Finn declared, eyebrows bouncing up and down like a pair of hedgehogs on springs. "Now, little..?"

"Brownie sir," the little rabbit offered Finn.

"Now, little Brownie," he smiled. "Hop up on my back and you too Jeffrey. We'll get to that burrow to sort those weaselly rascals out and on the way tell me everything you know. Once we get there, we'll see some action, all right!"

"Hang on, old boy," Jeffrey turned to Finn, "If there's action, might one put one's teeth in?"

Finn sighed, "O.k. - go and fetch them but hurry up will you."

"Thanks old bean," Jeffrey called over his shoulder as he hopped over a low part of the wall into the next garden. He popped back a minute or so later, sporting a rather fetching set of huge, sharp gnashers that might have been a couple of sizes too big (at least!). "These are my biting teeth. Don't get much chance to use them these days," he told Brownie, struggling to get the words around the enormous fangs.

Brownie hung onto Finn's shoulder fur and Jeffrey clung onto his back as, emitting a loud cry of, "Tally Ho" the deerhound set off, clearing the wall and roaring off like a huge hairy missile into the woods. Anyone walking in the wood that morning would have gasped with surprise at the sight of a vast shaggy deerhound galloping past and on top a little rabbit with her eyes shut tight and an elderly ginger cat with two mouthfuls of teeth crammed in his jaws, bouncing around, cheering and singing loudly as he tried to cling on.

As they went, Brownie explained about the way she had escaped, where the entrances were and about the large doorway which was Rubbish's. She told them about where the fox was sleeping, where the weasels were holding the rabbits and where Rubbish was lying tied in the sack.

Flying through the woods they made terrific time – Brownie was amazed how fast the deerhound could run. They only had to stop once when Jeffrey was knocked off by a low branch and, complaining bitterly about his aching back and legs, he had to climb back onto Finn and they started off again.

Finn slowed down as they approached the burrow. "My dear, you'll have to be extra brave for us now," he told Brownie. "If you could go back into the warren the way you came out and see whether everything is still the same. I'll understand if it's too much for you."

Brownie flopped of Finn's back. She nodded and, summoning up courage that she never thought she had from deep inside her, she made her way back into the tunnel and crept down into danger.

In the main chamber the rabbits were still huddled together at the far end, away from the tunnels. The weasels were still there, occasionally shouting, "Boo!" at the already terrified rabbits to scare them even more. Vic had a stick which he was using to poke at the sack which held Rubbish. She could hear the puppy's muffled voice as he called out to the weasel, "Yeah, if you're brave enough, let me out and do that!"

If he did, Vic and Nev gave the puppy a big kick until he yelped.

Brownie nearly let out a cry herself but she put her paws over her mouth to stifle it for fear of giving herself away. She looked again but there was no sign of Max. Presumably he was still sleeping in Rubbish's bedroom.

Creeping back out she explained everything to the deerhound and his accomplice. Finn nodded in understanding and reassured that his plan would work he told them what they would do. He would make his way in through Rubbish's widened entrance (though it would still be a bit tight). Jeffrey would come in through the main entrance. Brownie would go through the side entrance and block it with some sticks so the weasels could not get out. Once she was ready she was to make a lot of noise (she told Finn she was a great singer and could make a lot of loud noise) which was when Jeffrey would go for the weasels and when Max came out of the side room Finn would deal with him. Brownie stared at the old cat with his mouth full of teeth; she didn't know about the weasels but the massive gnashers frightened her!

Brownie told them that she would try and get in and untie Rubbish but Finn insisted that she should only do that if it was safe to do so.

Finn pressed his way into the Rubbish's doorway – he could smell the fox from here already, and the stink of those musty weasels. At the same time Jeffrey began to approach the main chamber through the entrance tunnel. He had oiled his teeth before the attack just in case they got stuck again (the last time he had used them it had been so very embarrassing). Brownie quietly dragged a bundle of sticks which she used to block the exit from her tunnel. She crawled towards the end of the passageway, ready to scream loudly once she got there.

Finn waited silently beside the doorway to Rubbish's room. The weasels had their backs to him as they poked and taunted the rabbits. One baby rabbit saw Finn and nearly shouted but Bluebell put her paw over their mouth. She was wide-eyed as she saw the enormous deerhound approach but she had guessed what Brownie had done. She just hoped that

Brownie was right and that Finn could be trusted. As she looked across at the dog's big brown eyes, and resolute face, she knew that Brownie and Rubbish had been right about him. She knew she could trust him.

Up above the chamber at the edge where the ventilation tunnel opened Brownie looked down at the deerhound. Finn nodded to her. She stepped forward and began to sing as loudly as she could. The effect was electric! The weasels looked up; Jeffrey launched himself forward, teeth chomping and claws flailing. Vic turned and caught a claw across his shoulder and a set of gnashers connected with his left ear. Nev was so shocked he just froze until Bob stepped forward and gave him a rabbit's left hook which laid him out cold on the floor. The rabbits surged forward and covered the two weasels and within a matter of seconds they were tied up like chickens.

Brownie jumped down and untied the curtain holding Rubbish who wriggled out. Just as he got himself free he turned to see Max sliding swiftly but silently out of the side room. Before Rubbish could do anything Max had grabbed Brownie and pulled her towards him.

"Not so fast, puppy!" he shouted over the sound of the rejoicing rabbits. A sudden hush fell. The rabbits stopped exactly where they were, as if turned to stone. The only sound was Brownie whimpering as Max tightened his claws around her shoulders. He grinned. "Untie the weasels and let them go!" Some of the rabbits muttered, and one or two began to push forward towards the fox.

"Watch it…" Max growled. He squeezed Brownie and she cried out. "I think we have the upper hand here."

"Let her go, you beastly monster," Jeffrey shouted through his monstrous teeth.

"Quiet, you moth-eaten old moggie," Fox sneered.

Just then something moved behind Max; he could feel the hairs on the back of his neck stand up as if they were trying to look behind to see what was there.

"Now then, my good fellow. I would be very grateful if you would unhand Miss Brownie, there's a good chap," a very deep but authoritative voice spoke. It was said very gently but there was the hint of a real threat behind it.

It was Max's turn to feel a shiver run down his spine and he swallowed in a loud gulp that echoed around the chamber.

He turned very slowly and carefully to see a very large and hairy deerhound bearing down on him. The eyes sparkled with a humorous glimmer but the sheer size of the dog and the edge to his voice told Max that he was not to be messed with.

Max made a big show of putting Brownie down and brushing the dust from her coat, and shooing her away. "Now, Mr…Dog, I think we can both get something out of this," Max spoke in his oiliest tone. "We can share out the rabbits, and I will even allow you to take that puppy with you."

Finn raised an eyebrow, "Oh? That's very kind of you, fox. But why should I do that?"

"Come on," Max coaxed, "You must enjoy bunny meat as much as we do." Max had indicated the two trussed-up weasels.

"Mmm, bunny meat maybe," Max nodded. The rabbits all looked at each other and felt uncomfortable, all except Brownie and Bluebell who both believed in the Mighty Finn. The deerhound grinned at the rabbits, "But only if it's in a tin. We don't eat our friends."

Max swallowed again; he could feel the colour drain from the red fur in his face. It was now a rather pale pink. Finn moved closer and placed a huge and hairy paw on his shoulder and with a slight press squashed the fox flat to the floor. Max could only give out a muffled, "Get off…"

The rabbits cheered! Rubbish cheered! Everyone cheered – everyone that is, except a squashed fox and two tied up weasels.

"See, I told you that Finn was ok, and that some dogs can be trusted!" Rubbish called out over the sound of joyful rabbits as they undid the rope that held him in the curtain.

"Quite so, young pup," said Finn.

"Hear, hear," agreed Jeffrey who was being hoisted rather awkwardly onto a group of rabbits shoulders. He had taken his teeth out now and two young rabbits were staring at them as they lay on the floor beside the old cat.

Finn looked down at the pressed fox. "But what are we going to do with you. I don't believe that you can be trusted."

Fox mumbled something.

Finn stood to his full height and held the fox upright, dangling him from his right paw.

Finn coughed loudly and Jeffrey called out, "The Mighty Finn will make an announcement!"

"I am the Mighty Finn, Lord of the Glen, Lord of the Streams, Chieftain of the Woodland and Protector of the weak." His voice thundered around and through the burrows and Rubbish thought it was probably rolling right through the woods too. "It is my decree that you, Max Fox, are banished from this valley, that you and your accomplices must go over the hill and never, ever, come back into this Glen ever again." Finn spun the swinging fox around and held him up to his face. "If I ever see or hear from you again, or know of you hurting any of my folk," he nodded towards the rabbits, "Then I will not be so lenient."

He dropped the fox onto the floor. "Begone."

Even before his paws hit the floor the fox was scrambling to his feet and leading the two weasels behind him (the rabbits had untied their legs) he fled out of the burrow as fast as he could go. Max might have been evil, but he was not stupid and knew not to take unnecessary chances. They never saw that fox or those weasels again.

After they had gone, Finn smiled. "Well, that sounded quite convincing," he winked at the stunned rabbits.

Jeffrey laughed, "Dash it, Finn, you even had me believing!"

Finn added, "Don't know where I got that

from…Lord of the Glen…"

"I liked the Chieftain of the Woodland bit," Jeffrey nodded.

The Lord of the Glen roared with laughter and the warren shook with his guffaws and the gentler giggling and chuckling of the rabbits, a rabbit hound and a cat. There was much cheering and dancing and Brownie sang as they celebrated into the night. Before it got too late Finn had to leave with Jeffrey to go back to the garden, as he explained that the Maid and the Butler tended to fret if he was out late.

Bluebell and Rubbish escorted the Mighty Finn and Jeffrey out of the warren.

"Thank you so very much for protecting us and rescuing us from that fox," Bluebell told him. "We should have listened to Rubbish and believed in what he said."

Finn nodded, "Indeed. The youngest of us can often prove to be the wisest."

Rubbish agreed, "And it's thanks to Brownie who believed in me so much that she came to find you."

"Quite so, quite so," Jeffrey added.

"Shall I hop up?" the cat asked.

Finn chuckled, "Yes, but this time I'll try to give you an easier ride."

The old cat clambered up (Finn knelt as low as he could to help him on) and shouting their goodbye's they disappeared into the wood and back to the red bricked garden.

Once again Rubbish was the toast of the warren for weeks to come, this time Brownie was too. He had asked her how she had thought of fetching Mr Finn. She had said that as Rubbish had such faith in him and she trusted Rubbish then she knew she could trust Mr Finn. Rubbish had felt very proud that someone actually believed in him. This was a fabulous feeling for Rubbish as no-one had ever cared before about what he had said or what he had thought.

Over the following months he grew to really enjoy going out to play with the other rabbits when running around the meadow but he found himself sitting apart from the rabbits sometimes, watching what they were doing, but more and more he was looking beyond the rabbits, around the edge of the field to watch out for danger. He found himself becoming the "Rabbit

Hound" that Finn had called him. Rubbish believed that this was his responsibility, protecting the rabbits that were in his care, especially when he was out with the younger or smaller rabbits. He could see further and clearer than the other rabbits, could pick out movement way beyond their limits, his hearing was clearer and his sense of smell was much stronger.

However, he was still growing and though life in the warren was generally fun, being a dog in a rabbit world was getting more and more difficult. He was now three or four times taller than the biggest real rabbit and he was developing less rabbit but more dog-like behaviour. The rabbits loved him, and he loved them as they were his family but Rubbish was coming to think that he would need to find somewhere else to live. He did not know what to do or where to go. He decided that the best person to talk this over with would be Mr Finn.

12 - A BIG DECISION

It was one lovely sunny afternoon that found Rubbish at the wooden gate. "Mr Finn?" he called out.

"He's having a siesta but I think he's expecting you, dear boy," came the voice of the elderly cat from the wall above. "Hang on, I'll be down now."

There was a thud and the sound of rheumatic joints clicking painfully the other side of the gate. Rubbish pushed himself through and there stood Jeffrey, rubbing his back. "Ooh, that's arthritis setting in. The weather round hear plays havoc with my joints, my boy. Follow me!" He trotted (quite nimbly for a crock of a cat, thought Rubbish) up the path, beckoning for the pup to follow.

Finn was lying on his bench crunching a biscuit and lapping milk from his bowl. He was wearing a pair of dark sunglasses (which looked spectacular on him and made him look like a film star). "Well, here you are my good fellow!" He smiled broadly at Rubbish and beckoned to the other couch. Rubbish hopped onto the couch and helped himself to the biscuits. Within a few minutes the back door opened and the Maid and the Butler stood in the doorway, watching the two dogs sitting there without speaking. The Maid produced a bowl of milk for Rubbish then turned round and as they closed the door he could hear the two people talking to each other.

"Mr Finn, I have a problem," he announced.

Finn looked at Rubbish over the rims of his glasses, "Oh?"

Rubbish nodded, "It's awkward living with the rabbits."

"Aha," Finn replied, "To be honest, I guessed that this would happen."

"It's not their fault; they're really nice, they look after me and they love me but it's just that… well..."

Jeffrey jumped in., "You want to do doggy things."

Finn frowned.

"Yes, that's right. They have made the warren really comfortable, I have my own room and bed, they watch over me (when I'm not watching over them). But the warren is getting too small for me; I need more room to stretch. I like to eat meat, which they find a bit awkward." Rubbish also frowned.

"That's all part of growing up, my boy," Finn offered. "But it's something I have been thinking about too."

Rubbish looked across to Finn, "Oh?"

Finn coughed loudly in his most theatrical way.

The door opened and the Maid stood there with something large, red and fluffy in her arms. She came out and set it on the grass beside Rubbish's couch. It was a large round and fluffy cushiony bed. "This is for you, little puppy," she said.

Rubbish looked at her and then to Finn and back again.

"It's yours if you want it," Finn said.

Rubbish felt his heart miss a beat.

"You can live here with us, little pup," the Maid said, "If you'd like to. There's a space in the kitchen near Finn's bed. You can keep each other company."

Rubbish sat there wide-eyed with awe. He did not know what to say – all he could do was smile and nod.

"But you will have to wear this," the Maid held out

a red collar. She leant forward and slipped the collar over the greyhound's head. Rubbish did not protest. His tail wagged and gave away his happiness in a way his words could not.

"Is this what you want?" Jeffrey asked.

Finn, the Cat and the Maid all looked to Rubbish.

"Yes please, that would be very nice but," the puppy added, "I will still watch over the warren as that's what Rabbit Hounds do."

Finn woofed and chomped at the Maid who seemed to understand what he meant and she ruffled the new arrival's head, then went inside, taking the bed with her. Rubbish could see her setting it on the floor next to a grey-check bed much bigger than his, which must have been Finn's.

"We can understand her but she doesn't really understand everything we say. I think they have put a name tag on it for you but they didn't understand when I said your name was Rubbish. I think they've called you "Sean"," he said.

Rubbish thought for a little bit, then nodded and declared, "Sean….that's a nice name for the people to use but to everyone else I'll always be Rubbish."

Rubbish went back to the warren to tell them he would be leaving and moving in with the Mighty Finn in the house at the end of the garden. The rabbits were all sad; especially Bluebell who gave him a big hug and her tears dripped off her chin and ran down his shoulder as she gave him a hug. This was very difficult now as Rubbish was so tall. Being very brave, Rubbish tried not to cry himself but he could not help having very watery eyes too. He promised that he would still visit every day to see that everyone was safe and the rabbits were to understand that he was still a rabbit hound and that if they ever had any problems that needed his help they were to come and fetch him immediately.

That night in the kitchen of the house he ate from his own bowl next to Finn's, and as the sun went down the lights in the kitchen came on giving the room a lovely warm glow, just like the glow he felt inside. Last thing at night he took a tour of the garden with Finn to do what dogs must do before bedtime, and then they both returned to the warm kitchen where they lay in their beds alongside each other. The Maid and the Butler were there to check they were safe, the Maid taking time to tuck Rubbish into his bed and give him a pat before closing the door and going up to bed herself.

"You ok, young pup?" Finn asked his little companion.

"Yes thanks, Mr Finn. It's been a very strange time. From the moment that sack with me in it rolled down that bank things have been so marvellous and wonderful. I have a great family, and great friends. I think this is the best life in the world." Rubbish snuggled into his bed and, listening to the Deerhound beginning to snore, he too drifted off to sleep.

The Maid and the Butler took great care of the young greyhound. They were really pleased that he got on so well with Finn as they knew Finn could be a very rambunctious character that other dogs might not understand. They watched as Finn would lead the young dog round, the pup seeming to hang on Finn's every word. It was good for Finn too to have company. What was a bit of a mystery was where the young Sean would disappear to in the afternoons. He would be gone for hours but by tea-time, as the food bowls were put on the counter to be filled, there he would be, brown stripy face and black nose, standing beside the shaggy Finn outside the back door waiting patiently for his food.

One morning the Maid called the Butler, "Quick, you must come and see this. It's amazing!"

The Butler came to the window and, like the Maid, they both stared open-mouthed at the scene that met them. It was a beautiful sunny morning and the dew was still glistening on the shimmering lawn, but that was not the incredible part; what surprised them was that in the middle of the lawn sat Finn, Sean and the old cat from next door. That too was not so unusual. What was were the seven or eight young rabbits that ran around them, scampered over Sean's feet and one, a particularly brown one, even sat on Finn's back. The dogs were smiling and even the cat was grinning, gummily.

Out in the garden, if they had listened, they would have heard the sound of the Finn and Rubbish laughing, the rabbits giggling and the sound of Jeffrey purring very loudly.

The dogs were smiling and even the cat was grinning, gummily.

13 - THE WINTER HARE

1 THE LONGEST WINTER

Finn the deerhound was dosing as usual on his chaise longue in the garden. Beside him lay a large bowl of dog biscuits – chocolate flavour (not real chocolate of course as that is bad for dogs), a bowl of water and an empty dog bed. It was empty because its occupant, Rubbish the Rabbit hound, was nowhere to be seen as he had gone off on another adventure. Finn yawned; he liked the occasional adventure, but never before lunch if he could help it. The sun was shining on the garden, reflecting off the grass and the empty flower beds; the plants were growing slowly but it was too early for them to have opened their delicate coloured faces yet. Finn sniffed; winter was a bit slow to finish this year though by the look of Finn's magical garden you would not have known it. With his incredible hearing he could hear a commotion in the distance as something was coming closer and in a very noisy hurry.

He looked up towards the tall door at the far end of the garden, the one that opened onto the meadow and then the deep wood. He could make out a nose pushing through and then shoulders and with a "plop!" out sprang Rubbish as he sped down the garden towards Finn. He had a wet puddle on the bridge of his nose.

"Mr Finn! Mr Finn!" he called as he skidded to a halt on the lawn in front of the huge grey shaggy deerhound. "The woods are all white and it's really cold and it makes my feet hurt."

Finn smiled, "What ho, my young pup? What are you talking about?"

Again Rubbish babbled, "Really cold stuff, on the ground, in the trees, it's wet," he was panting and puffing with excitement. "I even brought some to show you – look, here on my nose". His eyes crossed as he tried to point out the wet patch on his nose.

Finn laughed, "I fear there's nothing there, Rubbish, just a puddle of water."

Rubbish sighed loudly in disappointment and sat down, "Aw…I really wanted to show you. It must have fallen off my nose."

"Not to worry, my boy. I think it must have melted, which gives me a clue as to what is happening outside the garden." Rubbish looked at the deerhound in awe, mouth open. "I think it must have snowed outside and that's what the white stuff is. Just snow."

Rubbish was even more in awe, "You're so clever Mr Finn." He paused. "But why is the snow outside the garden and not in here?"

"Ah, that my boy, is because," his brow wrinkled and he leant in closer to Rubbish,"- this garden is magic! It cannot snow in here."

The little rabbit hound was now so amazed he thought he would burst. "Cor!" was all he could say. He lay at the deerhound's feet to catch his breath, still a bit upset that the lump of snow had seen fit to melt and disappoint him so much.

Finn knew that the lack of snow was not magic, it was something to do with it being a high walled garden and facing south…or was it west…anyway he'd heard the Butler telling the Maid some time ago. It could snow in here but it very rarely did. However, this long winter was never ending and it was only a matter of time before the snow came inside. When would it be over and spring come? A better question was - why was it lasting so long?

Across the wood, at the same time that Rubbish and Finn were talking, two very curious young rabbits, Brownie and Scamp, were looking out of the main doorway of the Warren. Yesterday Scamp and Scutter had been helping their Dad Bob to clear some of the snow away but overnight it had snowed again and they could hardly find their way out across to the woods. "We'll ask Rubbish to help when he comes over later," Brownie told Scamp. "He's got big strong legs and can dig even faster than us."

Scamp nodded, "Maybe Finn will come too and he's got HUGE feet so can shift even more snow."

"Talking of Huge Feet - what's that?" Brownie could make out some prints in the snow.

"Huge footprints," said Scamp.

Brownie shook her head, "I know that, thicky! But whose footprints?"

They seemed to have come from the hillside away to their right, along the edge of the woods, and then stopped. They wandered around the Warren entrance, and then drifted off back towards the woods.

"Don't know what feet made these," Brownie said.

Scamp looked at his own foot print next to the strange ones, "They aren't ours. They're much bigger."

"They do look like rabbit prints though." Brownie examined the new prints and their own. "But made by a large rabbit."

At that Scamp laughed out loud, "Nah, the largest Rabbit is our Rubbish and they aren't his!"

Brownie whispered to herself, "Then whose prints are they?"

The person who had made the prints was standing not too far away in the trees, from where she quietly watched the rabbits. She was very tired and feeling weak but she was also very wary. She had lost some blood from a nasty wound but she had stopped it bleeding so that it left no trail now, it just gave her some pain and sapped her strength. If the rabbits had seen her they would have thought she did look like a large rabbit, with bigger ears and a beautiful white coat, except where the red mark in her side above her leg had bled – that part was a dark red. She knew she had to find shelter and food, and then she needed to get home. Winter was here and it was never ending. She sighed and looked up into the deep grey clouded sky - and it would not end until she got home. As she stepped back into the woods she wiped a tear from her cheek and it dropped onto the snow. Where it hit the snow it melted a tiny gap and almost as quickly a green shoot pushed through and burst open – it was a delicate little snowdrop flower...

"The Winter Hare" (The next in the Rubbish the Rabbit hound series), September 2018

14- A HOUND IN THE HOUSE

WHY A GREYHOUND?

I had never really been interested in Greyhounds. When I was a child growing up I had a dog who was my best friend and confidant. After my (later wife) Armelle and I got together we had often "borrowed" family dogs for their vacation. It was a treat both for us and for them for a few weeks a year – all had been large dogs, Old English sheepdogs, French sheepdogs (Briards) – we had fun spoiling them rotten until they went home after their holidays. I suppose you could say that dogs ran in our family (though not actual "running" dogs!).

I can remember meeting a couple of greyhounds once when one of my mum's customers came to our house; I remember they were tall and rather bony but they didn't make any real impact. Or maybe I had just filed it away for future reference.

Anyway, back to the present; Armelle had gone part-time at work and my job changed to bring me only 20 minutes from home. This meant that someone was home 3 days a week, and that I could pop home for lunch on another couple. My Mam was lined up to dog-sit on the other days, so having a dog would now be viable. We then began to wonder what breed of dog to have. An Old English maybe? No - too big, too much maintenance. French sheepdog? No, this time too expensive, and should we really just line a breeder's pocket? How about a rescue dog? That would help get a dog out of a rescue kennel, and give a poor dog a (what we thought would be) good ome. That sounded morally acceptable. One day after returning home from work I was greeted with, "What do you think about a rescued greyhound? Apparently they have a horrible life," Armelle said.

"Where did that come from?" I asked.

"There was a piece on the telly about Annette Crosbie – the actress from 'One Foot in the Grave'. She was saying how these ex-racing dogs are often mistreated but make wonderful house dogs and pets."

Like I said, I had never really considered greyhounds but coincidences (or fate) came into play; someone in work reminded me that a colleague was involved in Greyhound Rescue. I spoke to Linda – the colleague in question – and she told me a bit more about it, gave me some contact details and we took it from there. Apparently the Greyhound Rescue group she was involved with took dogs from the South Wales tracks or from Ireland. They had dogs across the area in rented kennels or in "foster" homes. When a dog was taken into rescue they usually went into a kennels but they need to be assessed as to their temperament, how they behaved, whether they were housetrained, how they got on with people, small dogs or cats. This can best be done by taking the dog into a real home, to spend time with a family and see how they adjust and what their needs are. This is an important part of the adoption process as it gives the adopter a better view of the dog, and helps to match adopter and adoptee.

We were told that before we could be

accepted to take on a greyhound we had to have a "home check" to see whether our property was practical, and whether we would 'cut the mustard' as greyhound parents. Prior to the home check there was a panic over whether we should clean the house or leave it "lived in" (I can't remember what we eventually decided but it was probably the "lived in" look that won). The couple who came to "vet" us arrived with a surprise visitor; we had our first meeting with a greyhound face to face. His name was Oddjob and he arrived with his owners Pauline and Rob. He was a (mostly) black dog, tall, thin but muscular – what in an American noir novel would be termed "rangy". The obvious question was "Why Oddjob?" Rob said that he had been christened this because when he had been in his foster home he had been pretty clean but that he had left a "present" on his first time alone.

My wife as I said before was already sold on the idea of a rescue greyhound and after meeting Oddjob, I too was sold. (OK - Cliché time) - If any dog could be noble, then this dog was. He was quiet,

,a strong silence with eyes that looked so very sad and so very deep. As he sat there you could imagine his forbears lying at the feet of ancient kings and lords in castles and palaces. However, his wasn't such a noble tale; it was a sad story of abuse, neglect but eventual rescue and release.

Some dogs are with their foster parents a short time whilst others never leave (they call these "failed fosters"); Rob and Pauline, I found out later, had four dogs that arrived, found a niche and never left. Imagine taking home an emaciated, beaten, frightened bag of bones and then bringing it back to become a settled, more confident bundle of muscles, legs and licky tongue. Once you build that initial bond it is difficult to break it.

But what about a dog of our own? How did we score on the "safe to have a greyhound" front? Yes! We passed the home check - another hurdle over – one step closer to having a hound of our own.

Over the next few weeks there was much frantic Internet searching for information on coping with a rescued dog and what to expect when you get them home. Many websites were scoured, notes taken and a scrapbook compiled. Armed with this and new-found confidence the following August Bank Holiday Monday found us ("us" being my wife and I and our young nephew John) arriving (late, as usual), skidding into the Greyhound Rescue Show at Pembrey Country Park just as people were starting to leave. Rob and Pauline and Lynda pointed out two prospective dogs. Fortunately for them but not for us, one, a black dog, had been homed that week.

Another dog standing with two children caught my eye. She was tall, taller than most of the other greyhounds we had seen, white and fawn - like a Jack Russell on stilts and steroids. She was "smiling" broadly, a yellow bow dangled loosely around her neck, pushed to one side by her head's perpetual swivelfrom side to side to watch the action all around her. This was that other dog; her name was Sally but, well, we were warned, she was a bit boisterous. You could see how excitable she was.

Game for anything by now, I took Sally's lead

and we set off carefully across the park. She allowed me to lead her as if we had been together for years (greyhounds are usually lead trained and walk well as they're used to being taken out in groups by the kennel hands at the track). As the four of us walked I could see that it wasn't just me that had fallen for Sally - Armelle was clearly already besotted. What really clinched it was the way that Sally allowed John to cuddle her, fuss her and to take her on the lead. Consider that we were all new to her, there was so much going on around her and John was squeezing her like a vice. She accepted it all without a murmur. We walked her back to the cars and then had a glimpse of that boisterous nature; two dogs were loose and running a few hundred yards away, across the park. Sally's eyes stuck out like organ stops, her ears extended like galleons in full sail and her body tensed like a spring at full stretch. Then she did it - she yowled a high-pitched tortured yowl and spun around as if trying to screw herself into the turf. I hung onto the lead for dear life but apart from the yowl and pirouette she made no attempt to escape. You can't beat your genes - three thousand years of breeding and track training don't disappear overnight. This "boisterous" outburst I supposed would also account for the dried blood on her cheek where she had become excited earlier in the day and had nipped her tongue! Still alert but calmer, we made our way back to our point of origin where Lynda, Pauline and Rob stood. As we talked I noticed that on Sally's right flank was a brown patch, about the size of an old ten pence piece where there was no skin and bare dark skin. I couldn't help but wonder what that was so made a mental note to ask when I got a chance.

That evening we talked and talked, discussing whether this dog would be the right one for us, should we wait for another dog…the discussion was endless and we went in circles like the electric hare. There was nothing for it but to have a proper "field test" so Sally came home for one day the following weekend as a trial. She travelled really well in the car, curious for the first few miles, watching the world go by but this soon got boring so she flaked out in the back of the car. At the house she was soooo quiet; polite, well behaved (though not understanding a single word of command!) and the day went well, apart that is from a minor accident on the living room carpet and the fact that she came into season on our kitchen floor! But hey, these are the joys and responsibilities of being a dog owner. She was so calm that we couldn't believe that this was a boisterous dog – after all, we were used to very big bouncy Briards – if this one was boisterous, the quiet ones must come with a wheelchair and a drip!

That evening we took Sally back to Phillipa, her foster mother, and said that we would really like her to come home with us permanently. The problem was my having to go into Hospital for three days in three weeks time, which meant that Phillipa would have to look after Sal for another four weeks. We felt certain that this wouldn't be satisfactory and had begun to resign ourselves to waiting for another dog. It was, after all, a real imposition to ask Phillipa to house and feed her for another three weeks. What a brilliant person – she said that she would look after Sally, no problem, until we were ready.

We can never thank Phillipa enough for her

patience, kindness and her very hard work. In fairness she had the hardest time with Sal; Sal was pretty clean but the final housetraining was done by Phillipa, as well as Sal's getting fully used to being in a house day and night. What was revealing about Sally was something Phillipa told us when we finally collected her from her. The window in her kitchen had a Velux roof window. One day when Phillipa went to open the window with the window pole Sally cried out and flew across the room to the furthest corner where she huddled, cowering and shaking. This had been enough to reduce Phillipa to tears and she sat with Sally for ages settling and reassuring her. What was equally distressing was the dog's fear that no matter how kind people were she was still going to be beaten. Sally had a fear of all sticks and umbrellas. Now we understood what the mark was on Sally's side – evidently one of her previous owners hadn't been anything like as kind as Phillipa. Later our vet confirmed that it was a stab wound.

The week before finally bringing Sal home had been a frantic one as we chased about for dog beds, bowls, and blankets and did more reading up on greyhounds. Many web sites provide invaluable information on what to expect, what you need to do and generally explaining how the dog views the new house. Expect a pool of wee, for example as the dog will feel insecure in a strange place and may have an accident which may be a way of making the house smell a bit familiar.

One of the recommendations was for a "martingale" collar, a form of nylon webbing choker specially made for sight hounds. Greyhounds, whippets and lurchers have necks that taper which makes an ordinary collar useless. With an ordinary collar the dog will see something, you will feel a tug and turn to see a muscular backside and tail disappearing into the distance almost as fast as the cat it is chasing. Likewise, chain chokers can hurt the dog and cut into their necks. As I was later to find out, a greyhound's neck can be very delicate. Most greyhounds wear wide leather collars but as we were to find with Sally, she couldn't sit comfortably or bend to eat with one on. So, a semi-loose wide banded webbing collar would be better. A lot of shop searching and web searching resulted in us buying a martingale collar from Austin, Texas. It was red, only $8 and arrived within a week.

Another old wives tale bandied about on the web is that Greyhounds don't moult (or "shed" as the Americans put it). Whilst this may be true in the US where many states have a settled climate all year round – this wasn't true in South Wales. Sally moulted in bucket loads, fine white fur, and a brush wouldn't touch it. The American sites suggested using a grooming mitt, which is a sort of rubber glove covered with rubber blobs. I can thoroughly recommend it - it pulls out the short fur, which can then be shaken off the glove. This proved to be a favourite with the local sparrows who collected the lumps of brushed fur off the lawn to line their nests. It was good to see that we were doing our bit for sustainability and to support the local wildlife! I wonder how thermally efficient greyhound fur is?

One thing we did find out from the web was what a "lurcher" was. A lurcher is the offspring of any dog that has been crossed with a greyhound. A lurcher is not a breed in its own right. They're usually border collie or Bedlington terrier crosses, used for hunting rabbits. There is also the Bull-Lurcher which is a greyhound crossed with a bull terrier. Greyhounds (or whippets) can be crossed with other sight hounds such as a deerhound or saluki and these sight hound crosses are called a "long dog" which is a particular type of lurcher.

A sight hound is any one of the hounds that hunts not by scent but by sight, and this includes the English greyhound, the Spanish Greyhound or Galgo Espagnol, Scottish Deerhound, Irish Wolfhound, the middle-eastern Sloughi and Saluki, the Afghan hound, the Polish greyhound or Chart Polski and the Russian Borzoi. There are many more sight hound breeds but these are the ones that come to mind as I write.

(Excerpt from ***"A Hound in the House"***, Crafty Dog Books Cymru, 2013, 2nd Edition, Jan 2020)

15 - FOUND A PENNY; THE MEMOIRS OF A CRAFTY DOG

ABANDONED?

The door of the van squealed open and I peeped warily out. We weren't in the city; there were no buildings that I could make out, there was only a wide sea of long grass.

"Out you come boy, time for a walk," the man said. He pulled a rope lead over my head and I jumped out onto the ground; it was soft and more than a little wet and my feet sank into mud. The door slammed shut behind me as the man pulled me away on the lead. It dug into my neck because I wasn't quick enough and a bit unsure about what was going on. I liked a walk as much as the next greyhound but there was something here that didn't feel quite right. I started walking, picking up the pace as he started to walk faster. The air was damp in the big field and I was picking up the smell of many strange things on the breeze. When I stopped to scent the air the man slipped my lead over my head and off. I was free.

"Go on then - have a run," he prodded me. I looked at him and then stepped forward. I started to walk, then trot and then I ran. It was fabulous to have that freedom to just run, to stretch out and fly across that field over the mud and grass, kicking bits into the air as I went. As I approached the far end of the field I began to turn and was going to head back in the direction I'd come from. I stopped; they weren't there. The man and the van were gone.

I didn't know what to do – I just stood there, all alone in the huge, empty field, panting from the exertion of running, just watching and waiting. He would be back any minute, I told myself. I slowly retraced my steps to where the van had left me. The gate it had driven through was shut and it was too tight for me to go through. I did manage to push my long pointy nose through the gate to see down the lane and I thought that I might have just caught sight of a van turning in the distance at its very end. He must have had to go somewhere but obviously he would come back for me.

I waited. It was damp, and the air grew chillier – I could feel the cold climbing up my legs. I missed my old jacket; it might well have seen twenty greyhounds before me but for the time that I had it, it had been mine. I told myself that he'd be back soon.

I waited. Birds began to gather in the hedge and trees along the side of the field near the gate. Huge black ones with long, sharp-looking beaks and straggly wings cawed at me. Some were braver and came down to sit on the top of the gate to stare down at me. Their cold black eyes, sparkling like ice, made me feel even more uncomfortable. I stepped slowly and cautiously away from the gate and made my way along the edge of the field. There had to be another gate, or maybe a hole in the hedge somewhere. When I walked many of the black birds followed me, hopping from bush to bush, all the while keeping up their constant screeching.

Still I waited. I was getting colder, the air was getting wetter and for the first time I began to feel scared and started to have doubts; what if the man had forgotten me? What if when he came back he couldn't find me – it struck me that being a black dog in a field that was getting dark he might not be able to see me.

I could see one distinct clump of trees taller than the rest alongside a pile of stones up against the hedge; it looked like it had once been a building. I continued towards it. The tumble of stones was still a shelter of sorts and I hoped that it would keep some of the rain off me – the icy rain that had now started to fall in huge freezing cold drops the size of my paws. I huddled tight against one of the walls to be out of the draught as the evening sky grew darker and darker. I'd prayed that the man would come back to collect me, but it was now that I started to accept that he was never going to come for me. I was on my own.

The rain beat on the rusty iron sheet over my head; it rattled and cracked as the drops hit it and slid down to land with a slap in the invisible puddles of muddy water that were all around me. I stood there all night, desperately tired but too scared to even shut my eyes.

At one point I could no longer hold my eyelids open and I must have fallen asleep. I was woken by a pain in my left back leg and I barked and kicked out - something scurried away into the dark. I never slept after that and I was so relieved to see the fingers of light pushing over the distant hedge as the sun finally came up after what had seemed like a year. When I looked down to my leg I could see that something had bitten me and left the marks of their teeth in my fur. It had bled but this had now stopped.

My stomach gurgled. When had I eaten last? It must have been the bowl of water and vegetables that I'd had before I'd left the kennels. Looking around the ruined building I could make out what must have been old food stalls for animals. I pushed my nose in and rooted through to find any traces of food but anything that had been there was now long gone. There were only spider's webs, mud and rust. The field was growing lighter as the sun had cleared the distant hedge. I moved carefully out into the open, back towards where I thought the gate had been but there wasn't a gate there. Somehow the night had confused my sense of direction. I went further out to the middle of the field. It was vast. I could see a metal shape on legs – it was worth a look as it might have food in it. Luckily for me it did; dried bits of food which were obviously not for dogs, but I didn't care - it was food after all. It tasted musty and the cake was stale. I shuddered to think how long it had been there, though the water in the bin next to the food was fresh, probably due to the heavy rain. It was better than nothing. Carefully, I went all round the edge of the field looking for a way out; I found two gates, one of which was the one out onto the lane. I knew I couldn't get through that one. The other gate led into another smaller field. Was there just enough room on one side between the edge of the gate and the stone pillar it was tied to for a greyhound to try to push through? No. The gap was too small. I sighed and made my way back to the other gate where I stood for a while, hoping someone would pass. Nothing. I turned and made my way back to the shelter. And waited.

This became my daily routine. I'm not sure how long for as the days merged, interspersed with black, fearful nights. Try and sleep with an eye open, then to the bin for a scrap of animal food and water, watch the gate, then back to the shelter. I found a patch of old straw at the back of the shed that smelled of another strange beast – again, I didn't dare to think what it was. At least the straw was dry. It helped me to conserve a little bit of body-heat in the dark evenings and overnight.

One time I heard a van in the lane. I managed to get up and even tried to run to the gate but I wasn't quick enough. I almost laughed – I'd been quick enough all my racing life but this was now my story; the greyhound that wasn't fast any more. I was growing weaker as the small handful of dried animal food and water wasn't enough to sustain me. I went back to the gateway into the small field and tried to squash myself through as I'd done for many days now without any luck. I must have been growing thinner because this time I managed, with a wriggle, to squeeze through.

It was yet another field but at least it was a different one. I trod slowly round the edge, keeping close to the hedgeline for two reasons; to look for a way out, but also in case anything unfriendly in that field wasn't too pleased to see me. The grass here was cropped shorter and there was a scent of animals that was much fresher than in the other field. The first field had seemed to have been as abandoned as me, but someone or something had been in this one recently. The green dropped away in front of me as I reached the top of a slope. This led down towards another hedge and gate – and beyond it, a group of buildings, noise and movement! I was excited, but now I was also wary. I went down the hill keeping the hedge to my left, moving slower as I was cautious but also because I had very little strength left to move any faster. I could hear a human voice the other side of the hedge, though further away. I halted and pushed myself into the rough grass and sticks at the foot of the hedge to hide. I was so weak I couldn't keep my eyes open - I drifted into a fitful sleep with dreams full of giant mice with blazing red eyes and huge, sharp teeth.

(From ***"Found a Penny – The Memoirs of a Crafty Dog",*** Crafty Dog Books Cymru, September 2019)

ALSO BY CHRIS DIGNAM

How Rubbish the Rabbithound Saved Christmas (*Crafty Dog Books Cymru, Dec 2015)*

..

Greyt Expectations, or From Rescued Greyhounds to Marmalade Cats (*Crafty Dog Books Cymru, Sept 2016*)

Printed in Great Britain
by Amazon

80363129R00079